Many thanks to Soto Zen

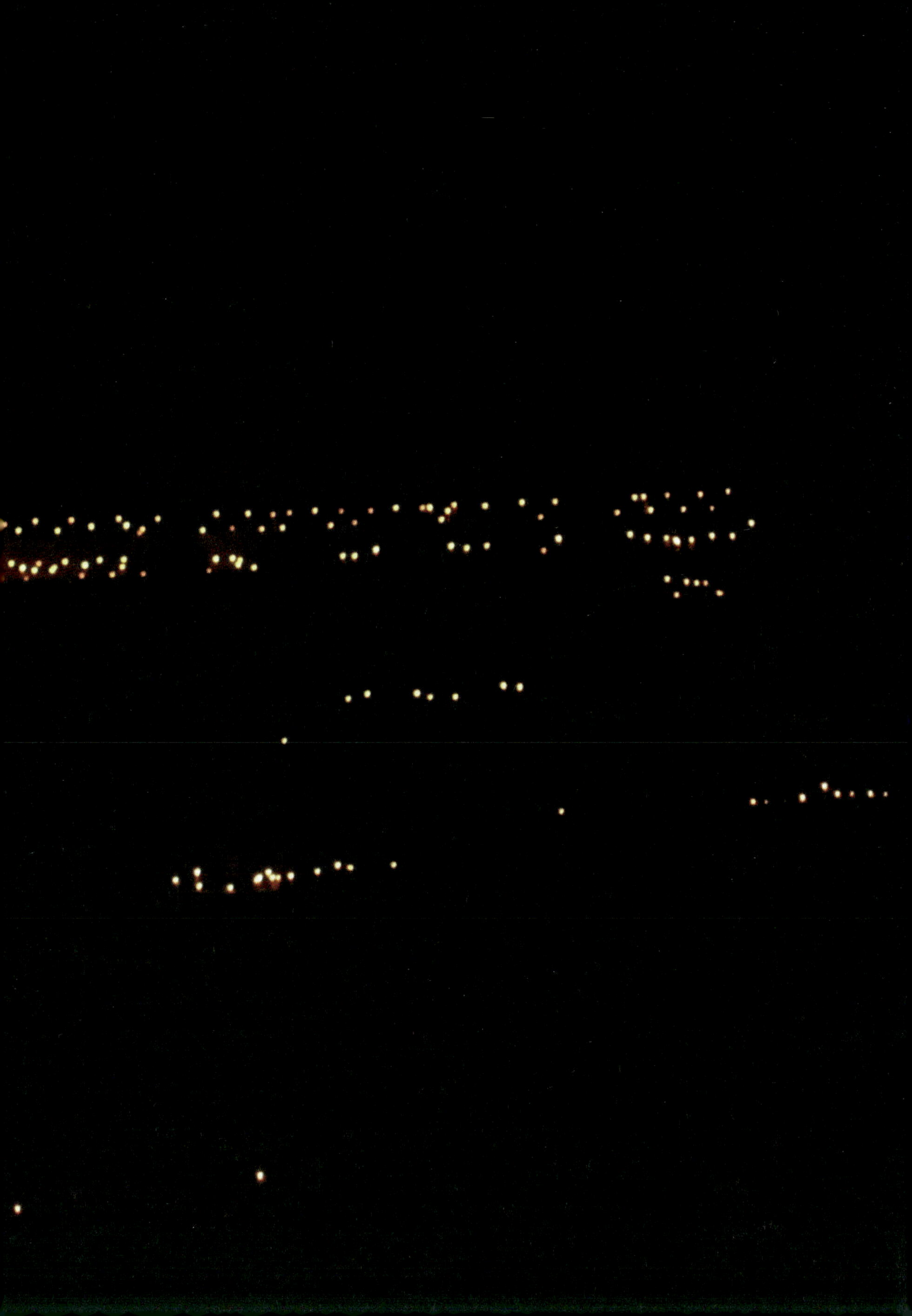

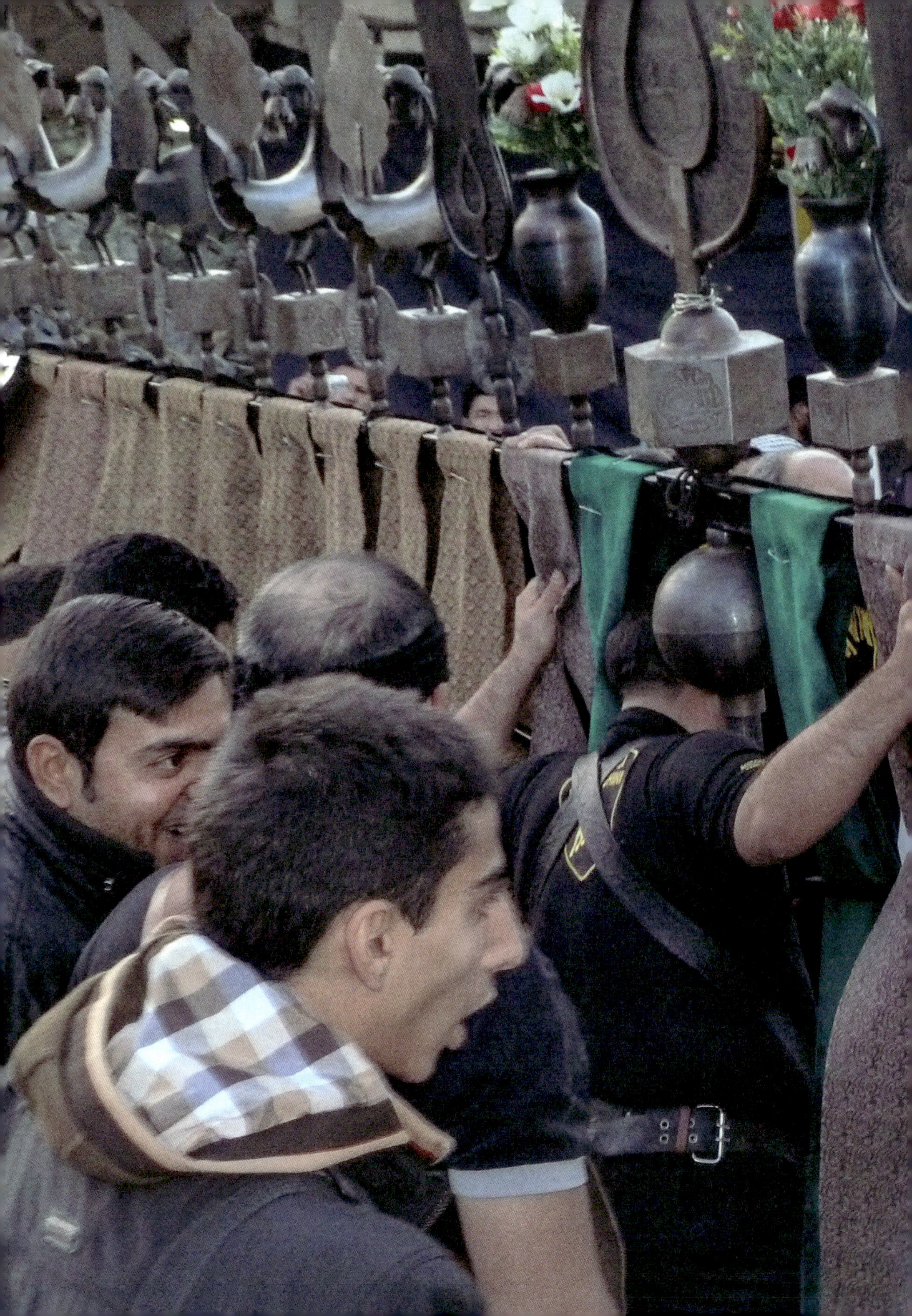

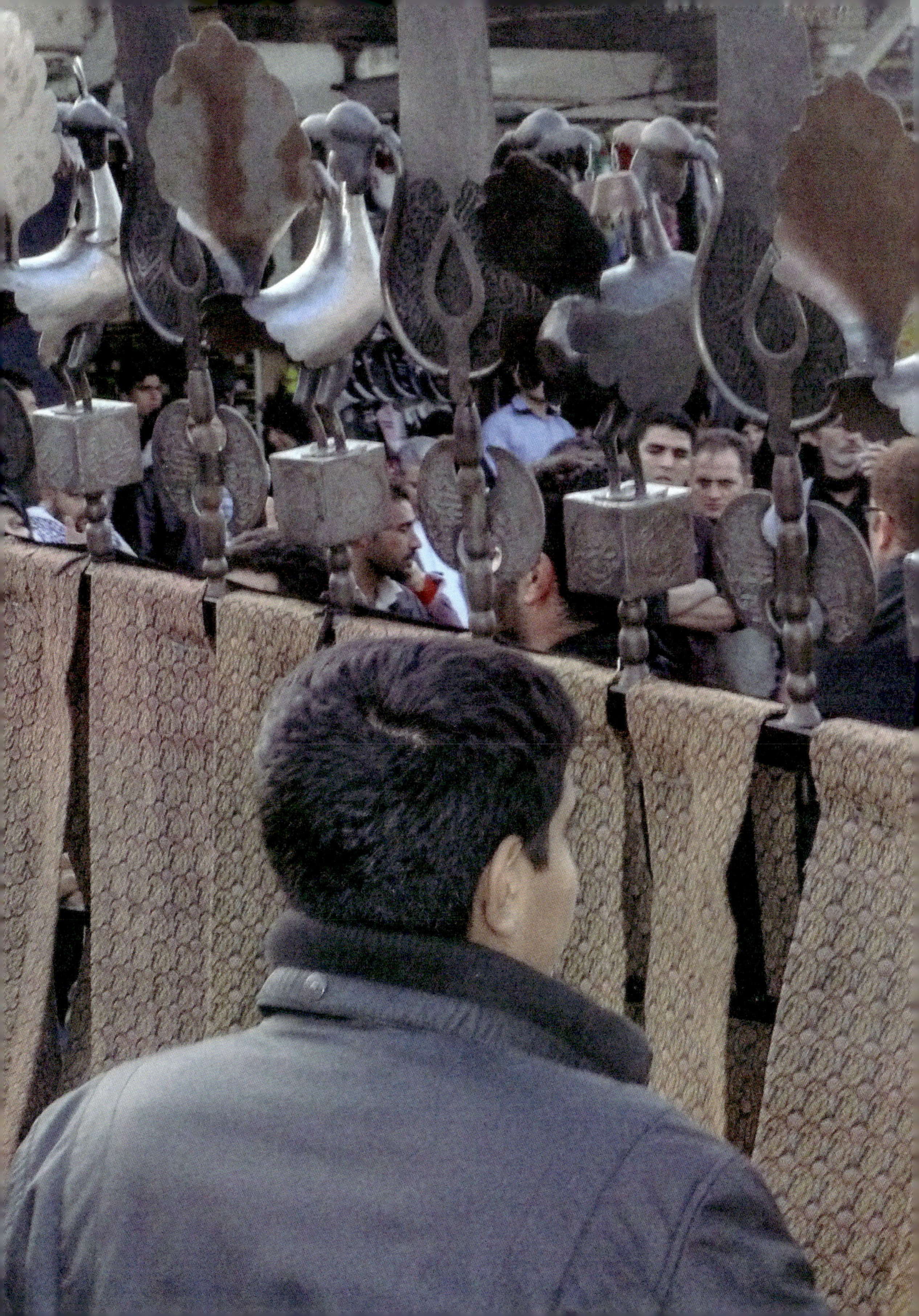

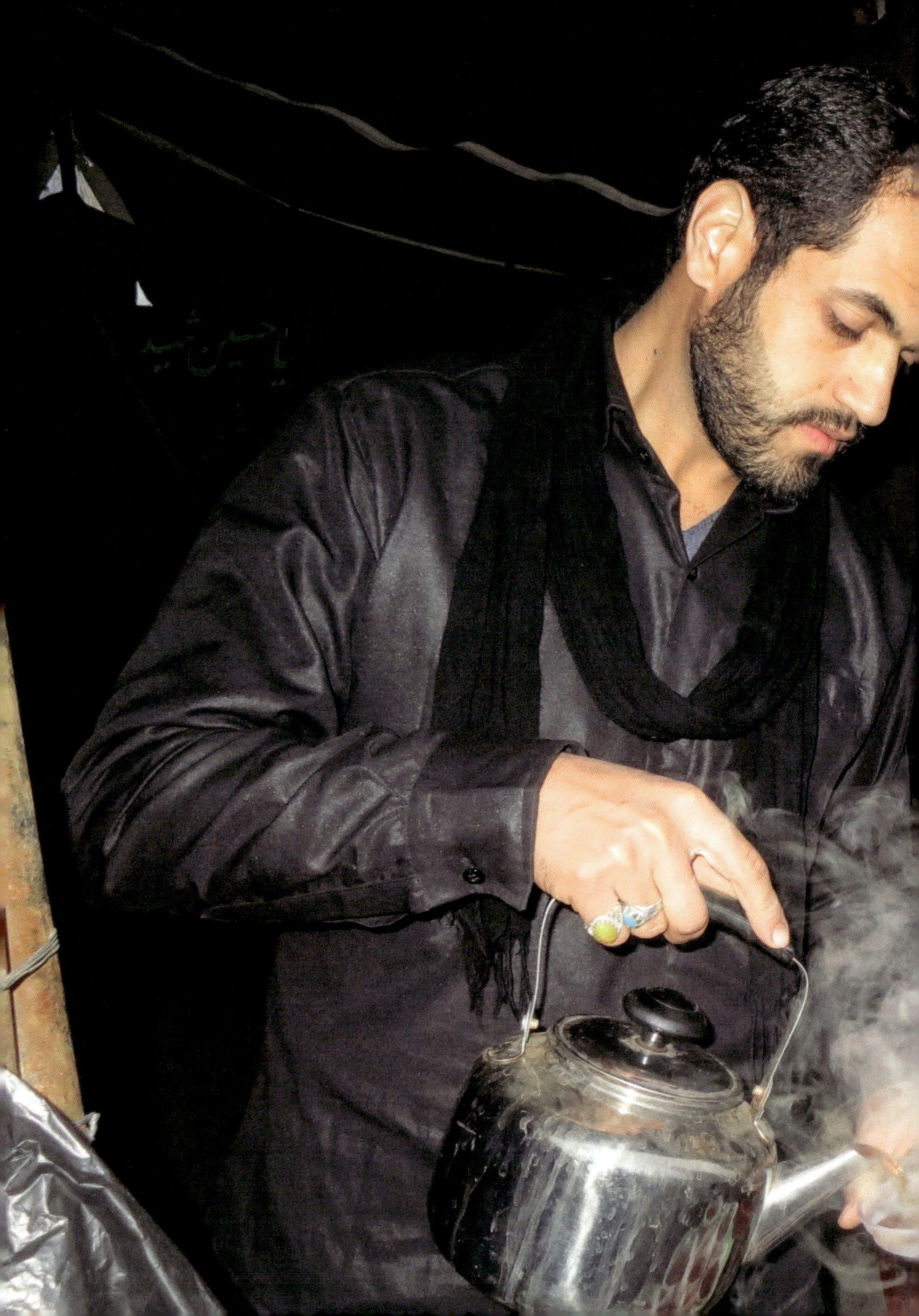
یا حسین شهید

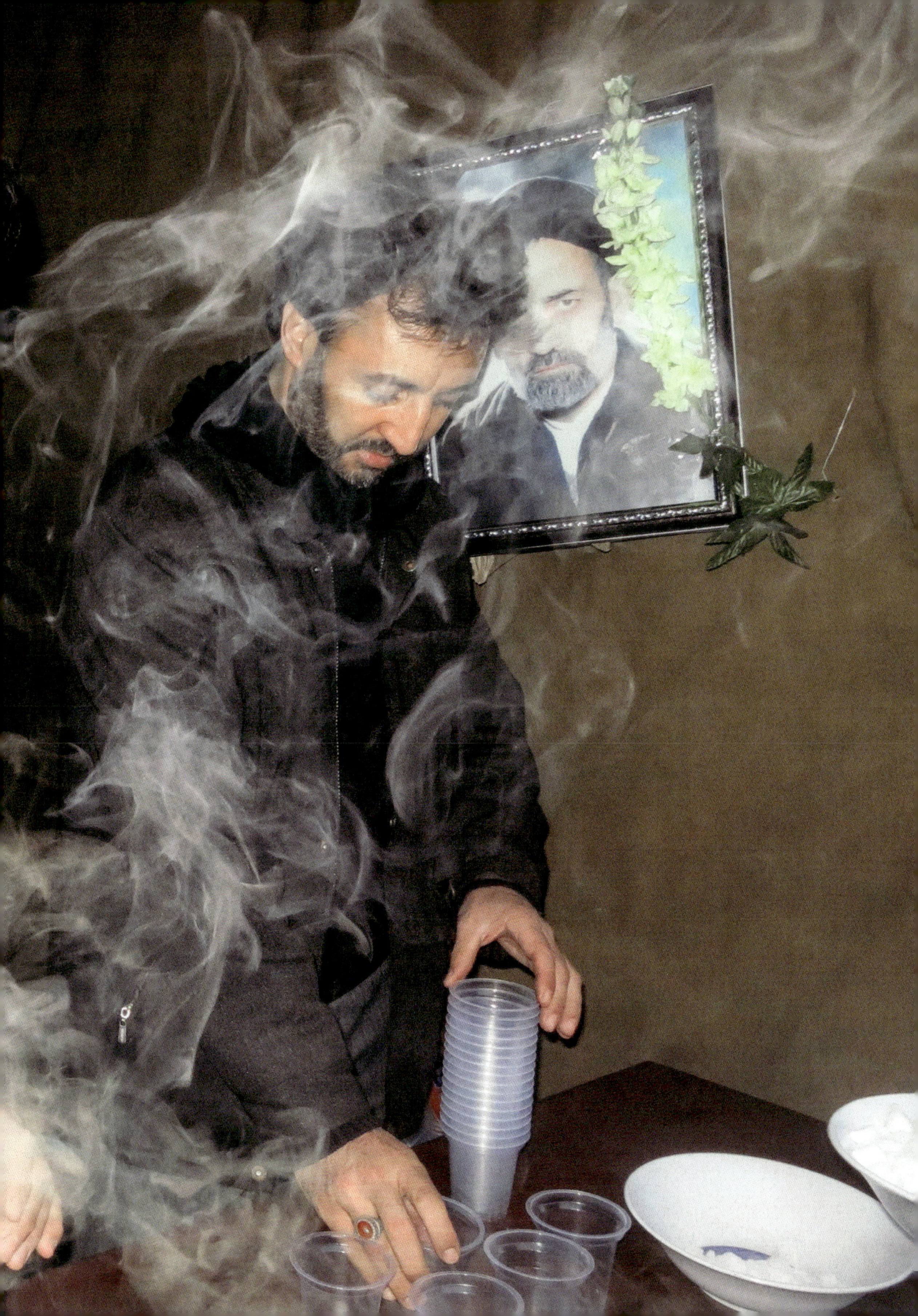

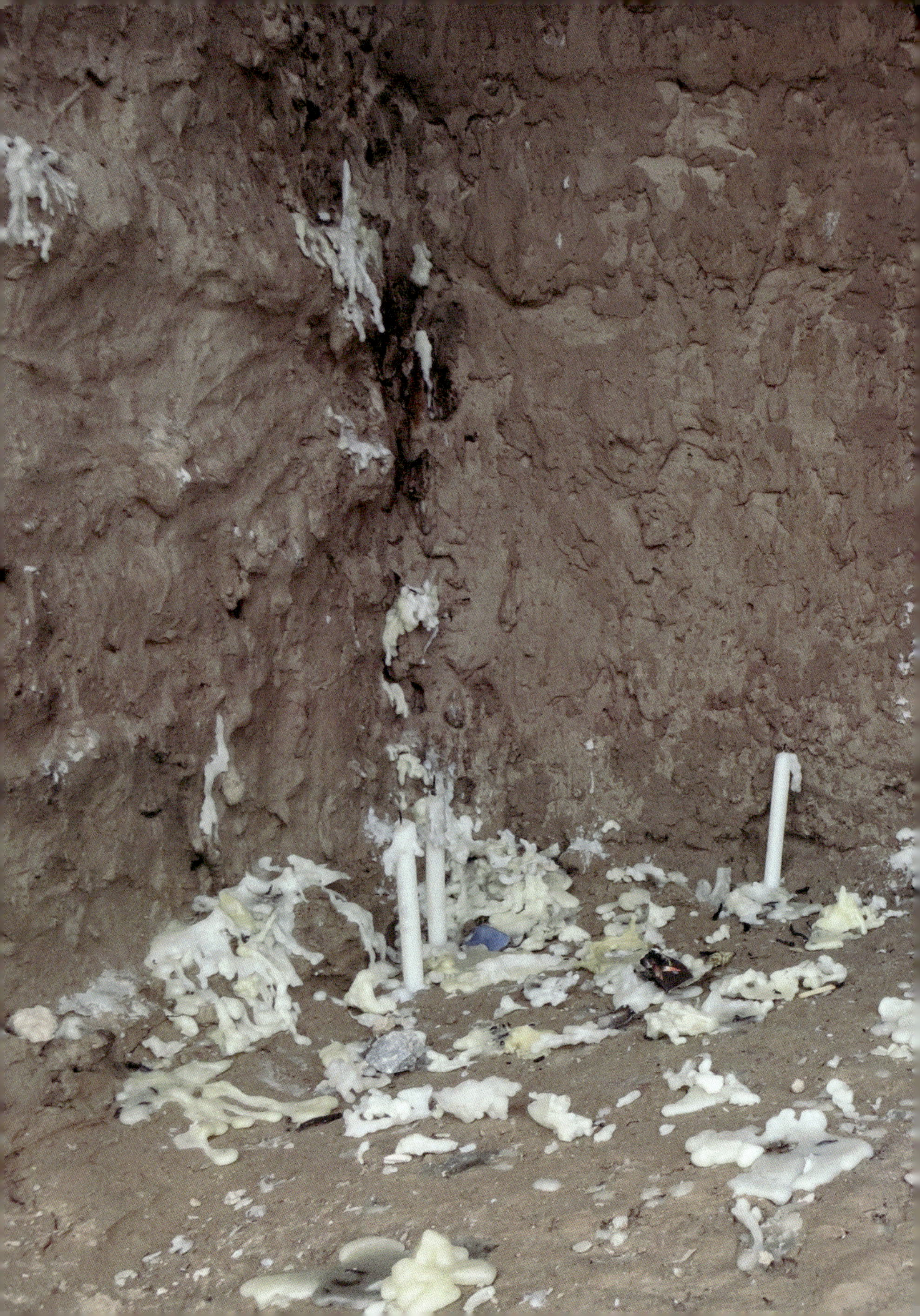

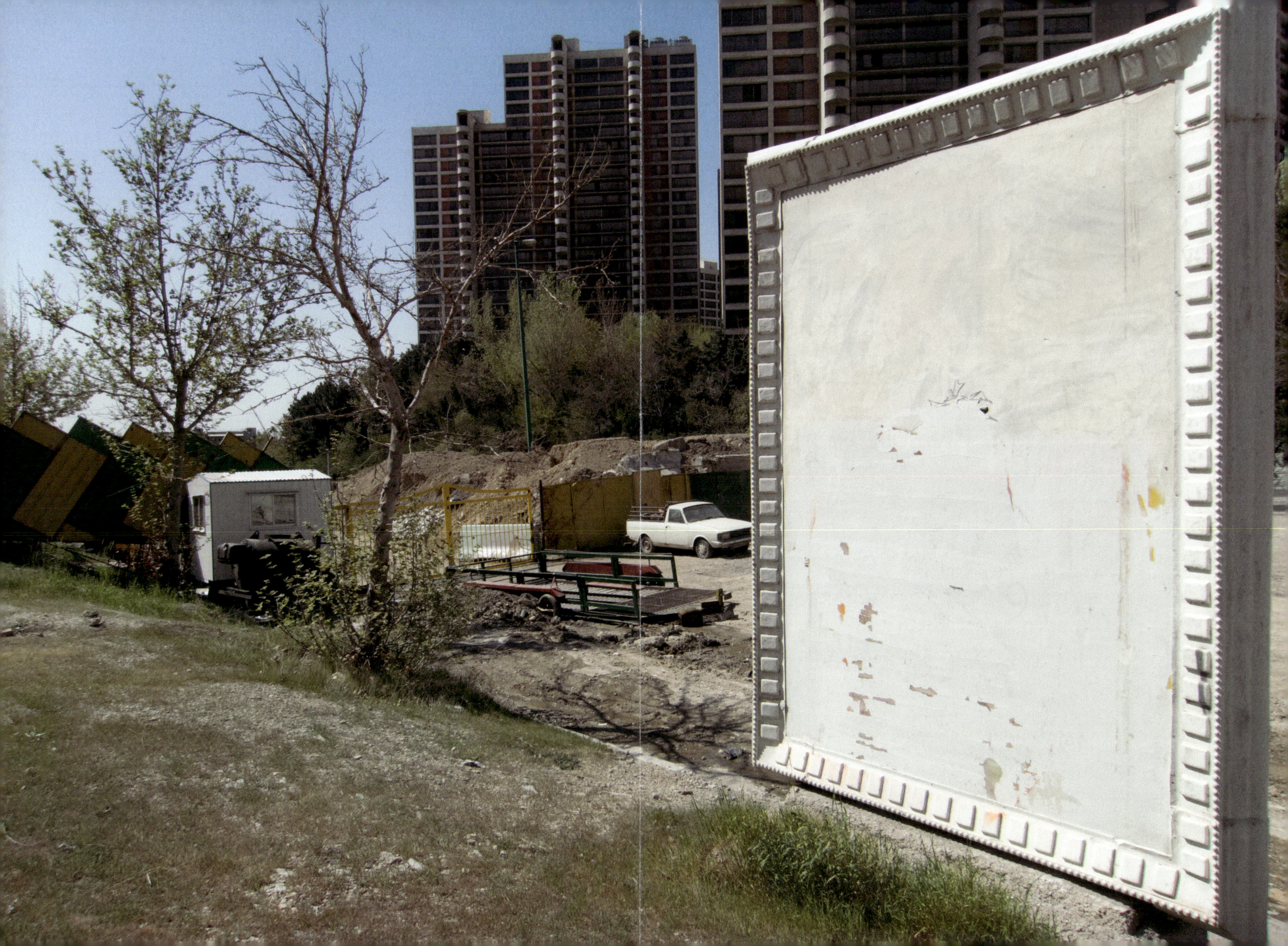

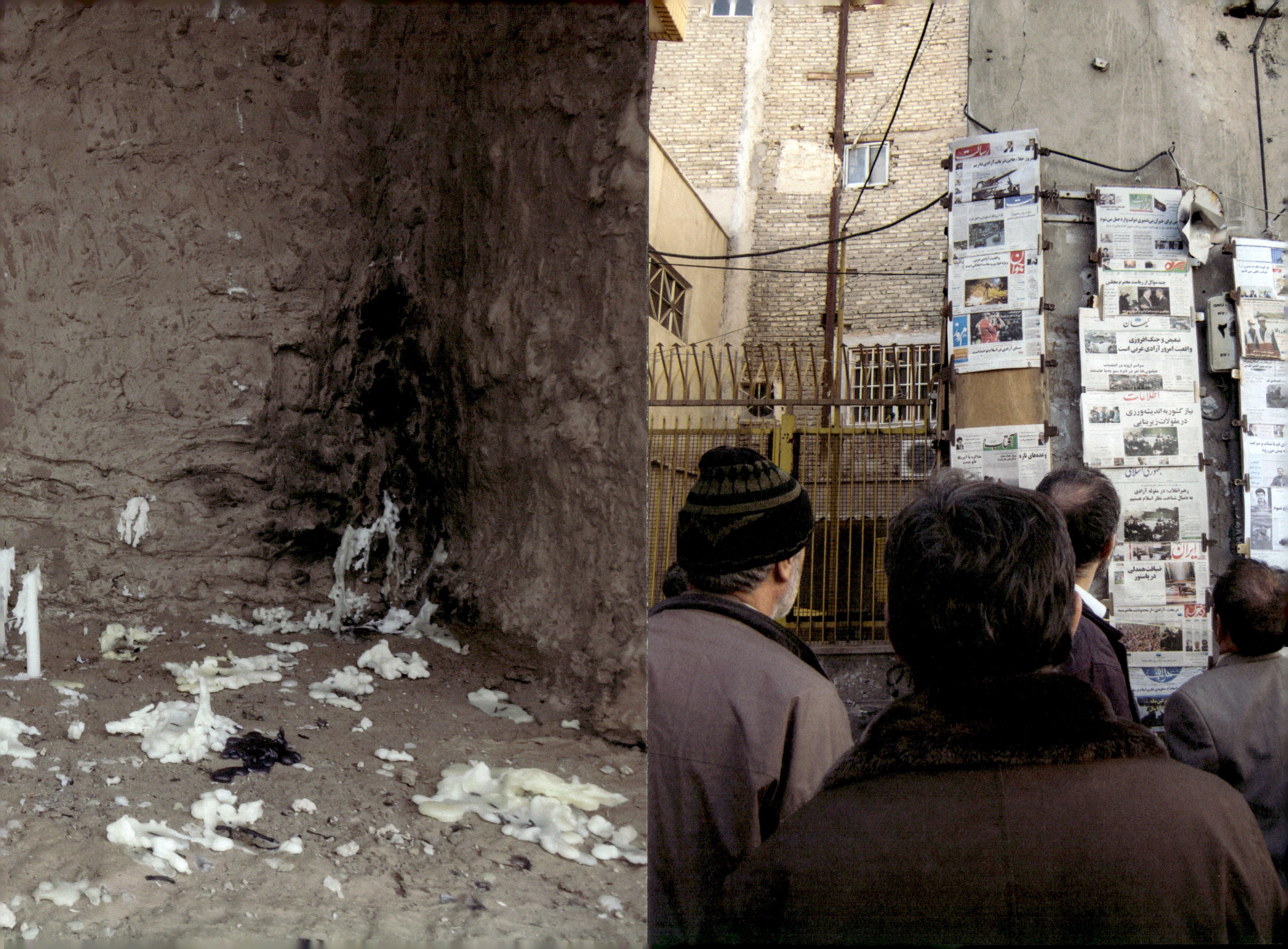

کیهان
تبعیض و جنگ افروزی
واقعیت امروز آزادی غربی است
اطلاعات
نیاز کشور به اندیشه‌ورزی
در مقولات زیربنایی
جمهوری اسلامی
رهبر انقلاب: در مقوله آزادی
به دنبال شاخص نظر اسلام هستیم
ایران
ضیافت همدلی
در پاستور

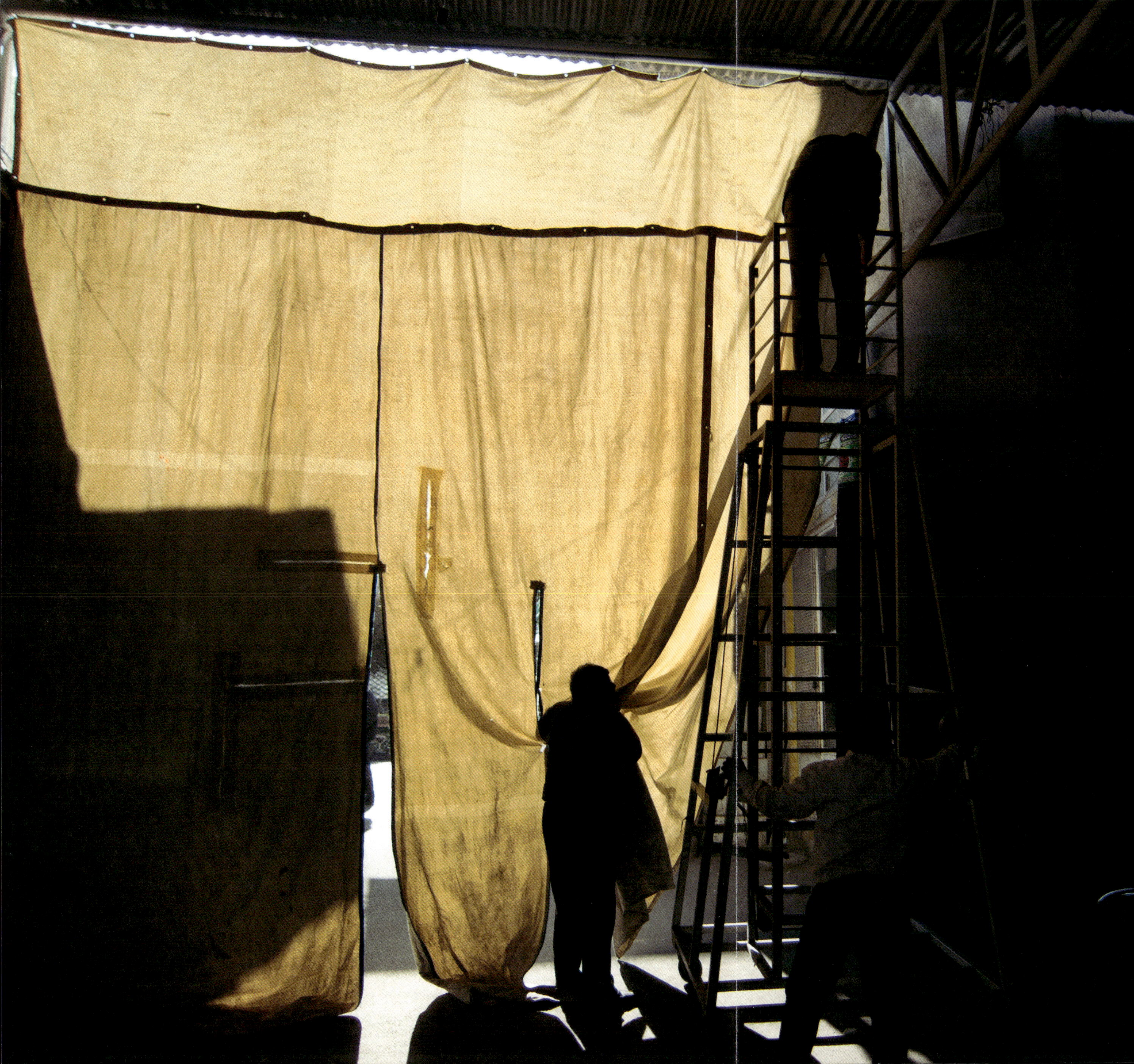

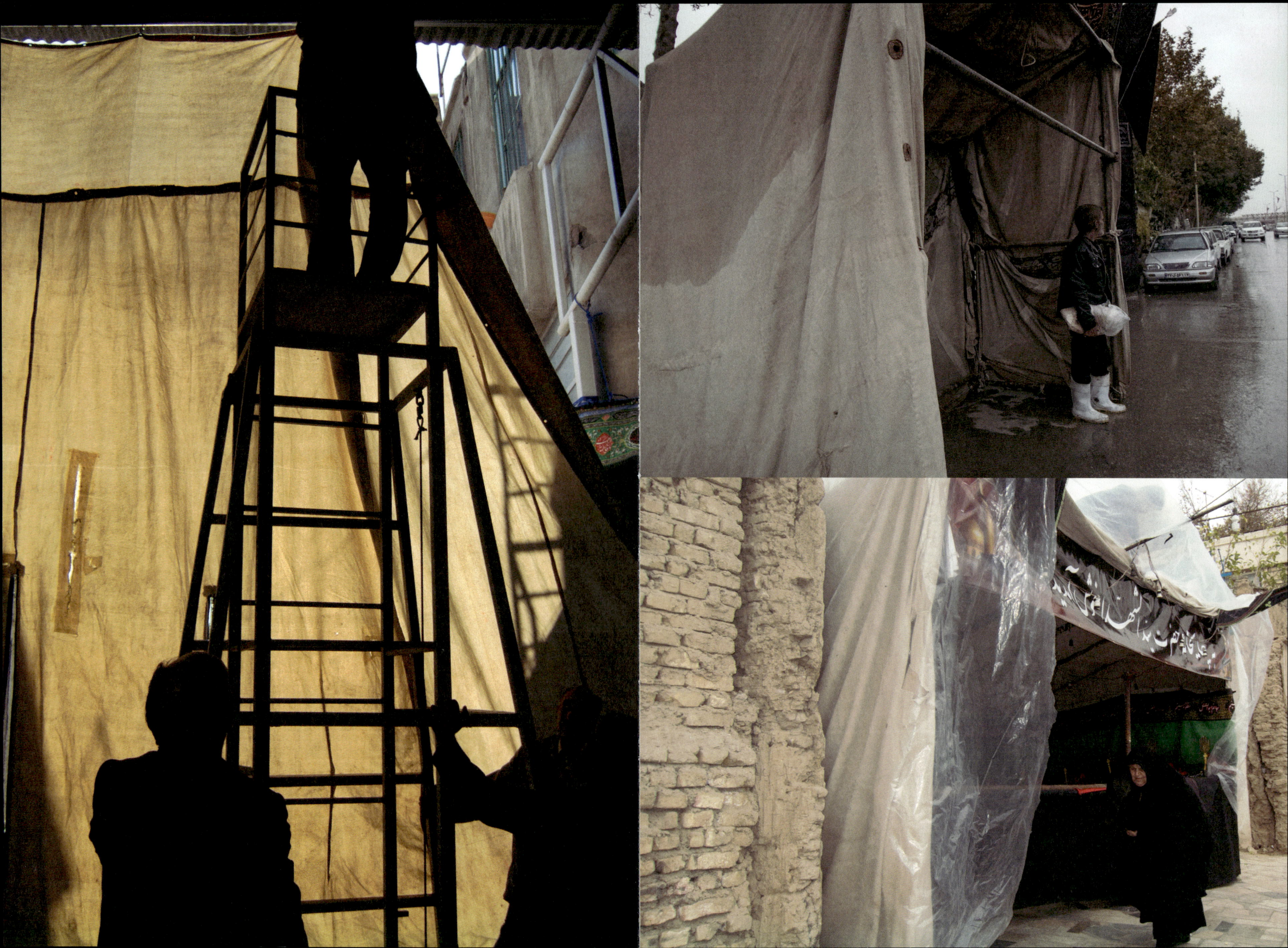

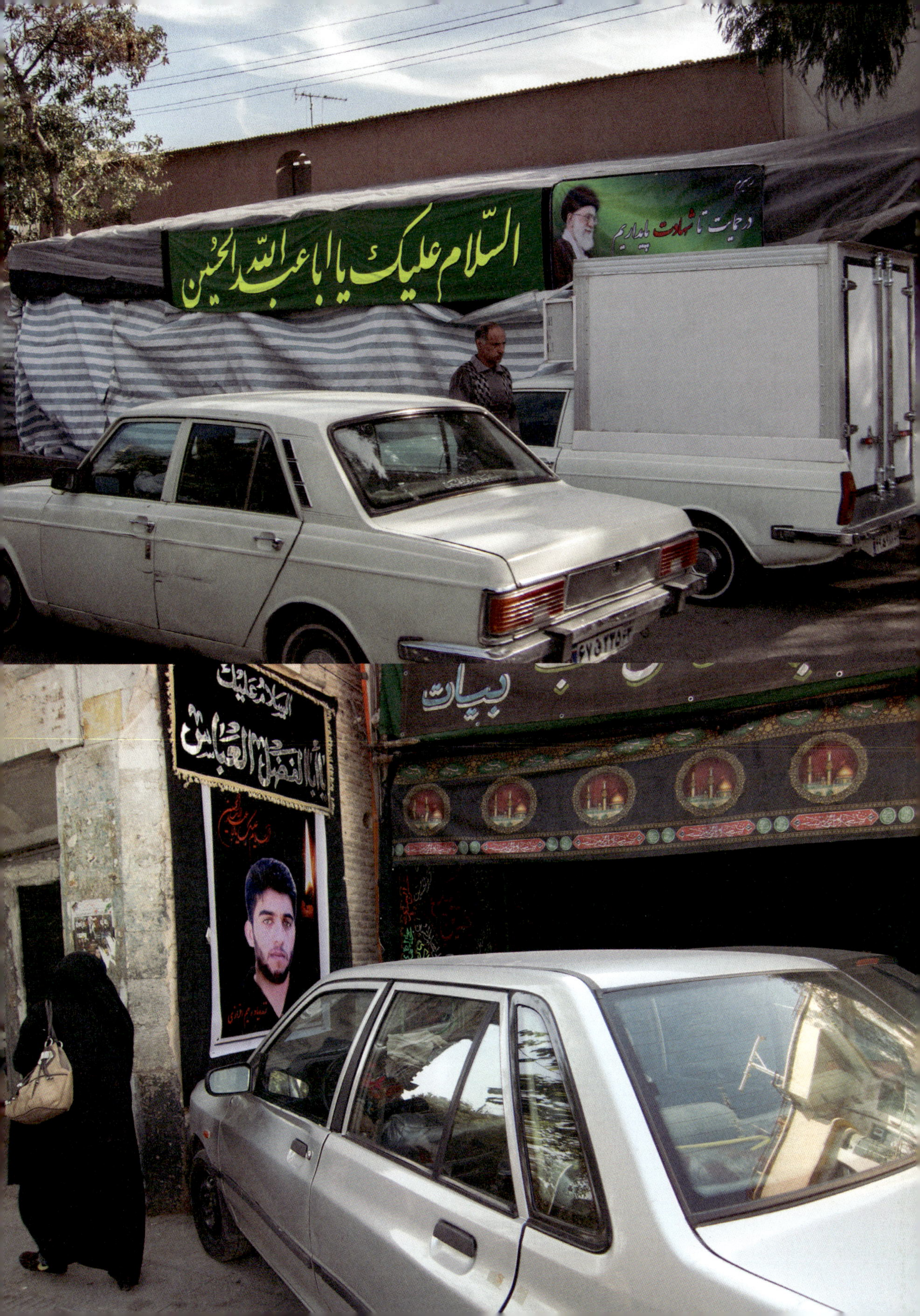

السلام علیک یا اباعبدالله الحسین
درحمایت تا شهادت پایداریم
السلام علیک
یا ابا الفضل العباس

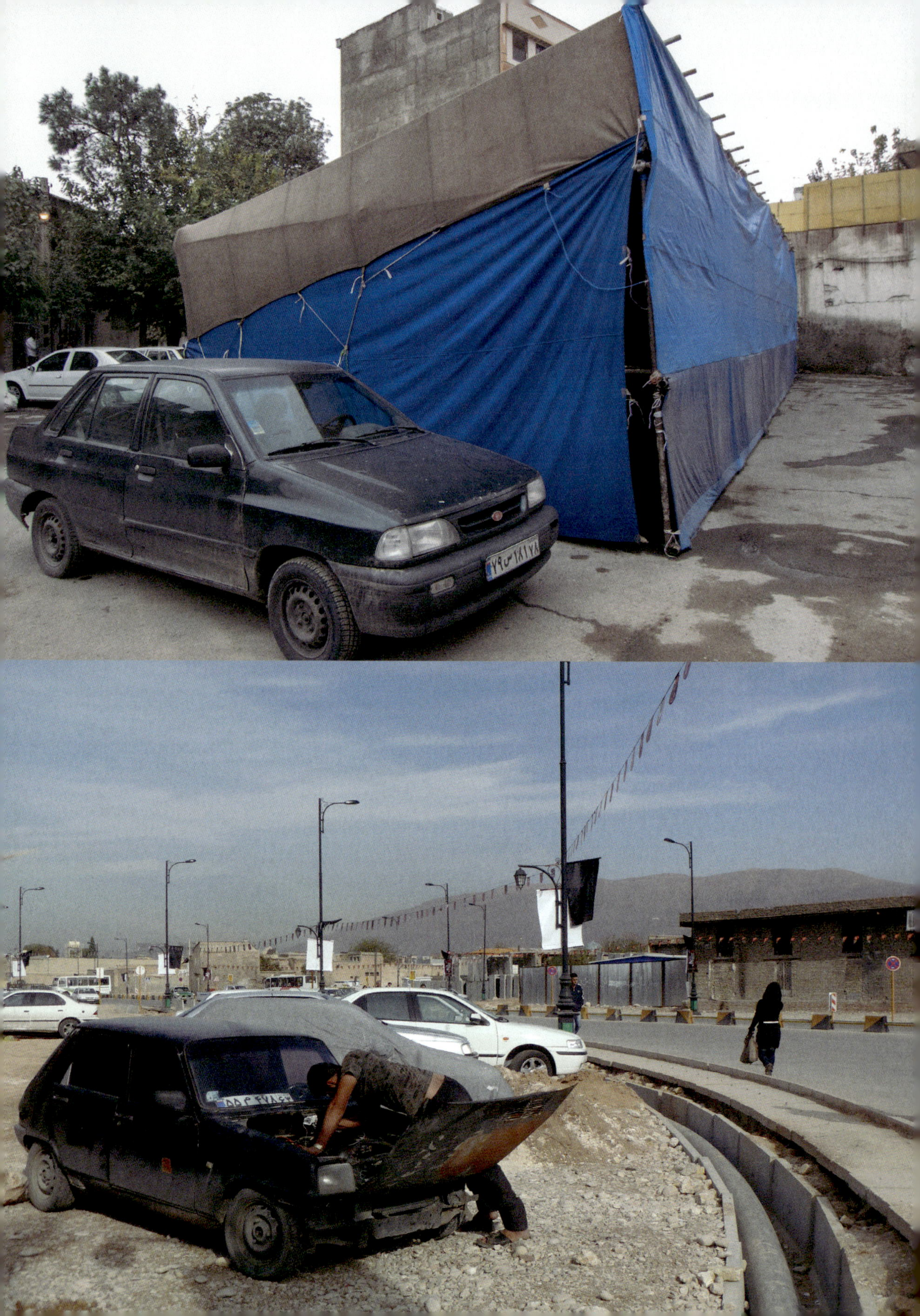

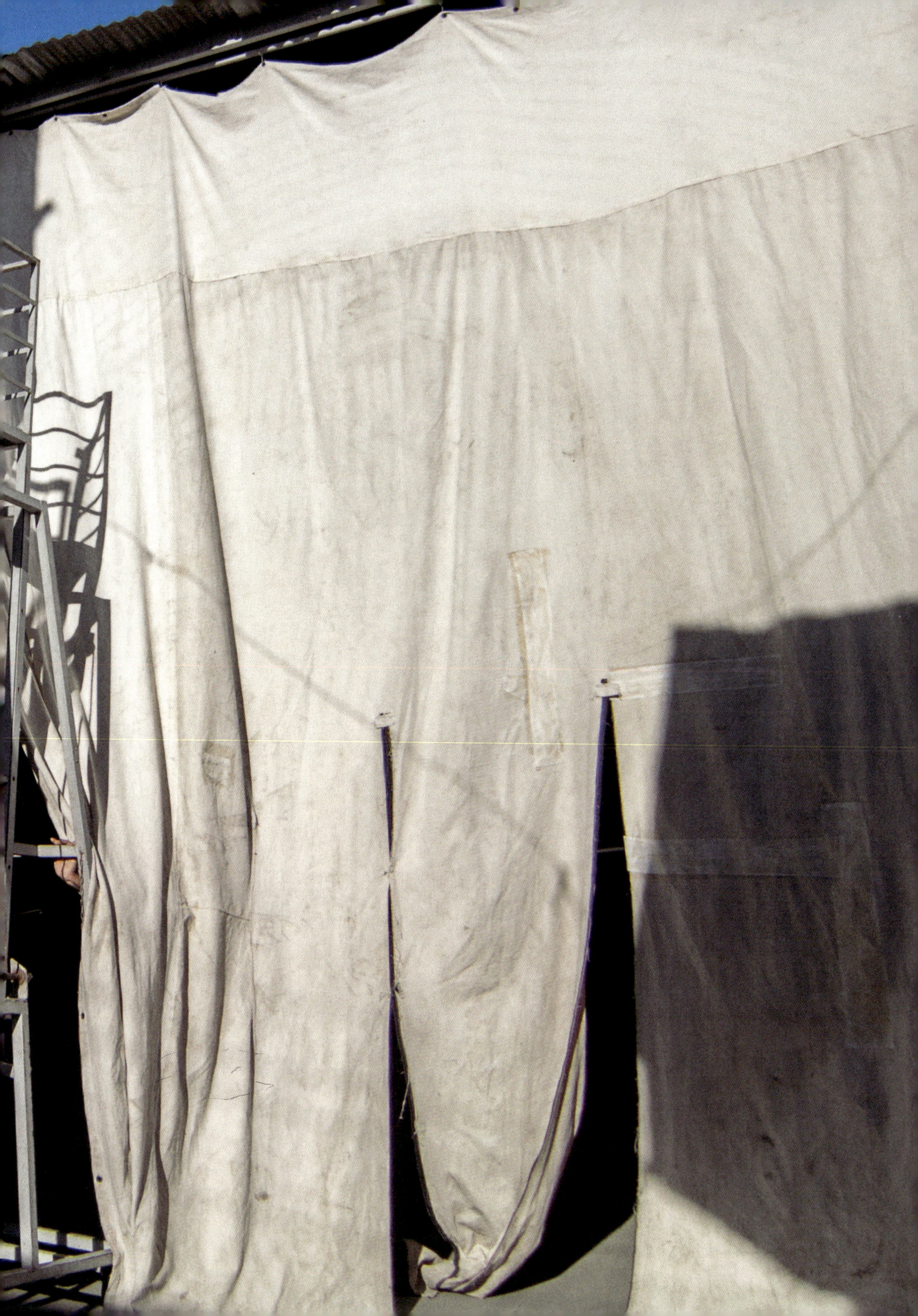

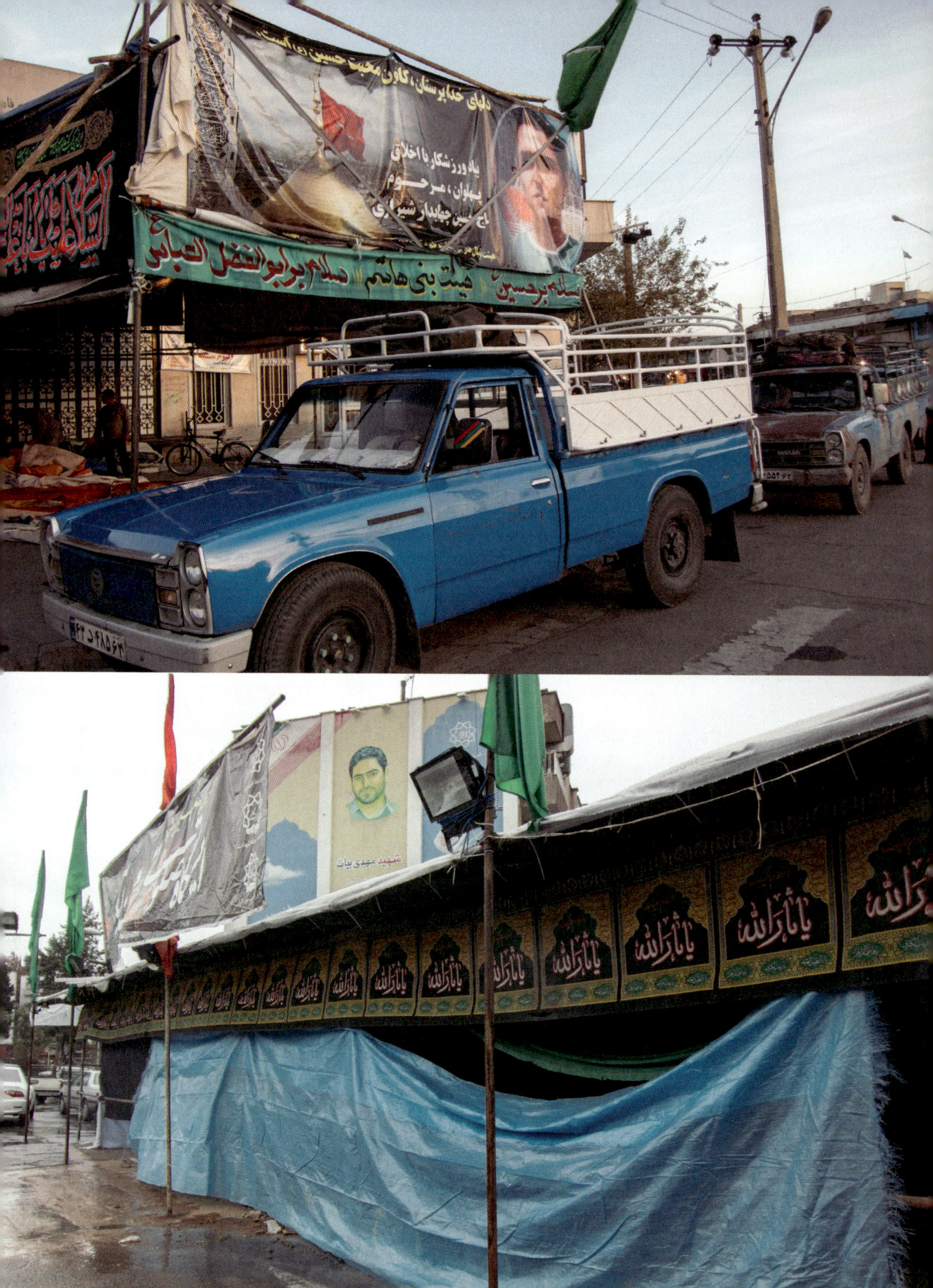

دلهای خداپرستان، کانون محبت حسین (ع) است
یاد ورزشکار با اخلاق
پهلوان، مرحوم
سلام بر حسین
هیئت بنی هاشم
سلام بر ابوالفضل العباس
شهید مهدی بیات
یا ثارالله

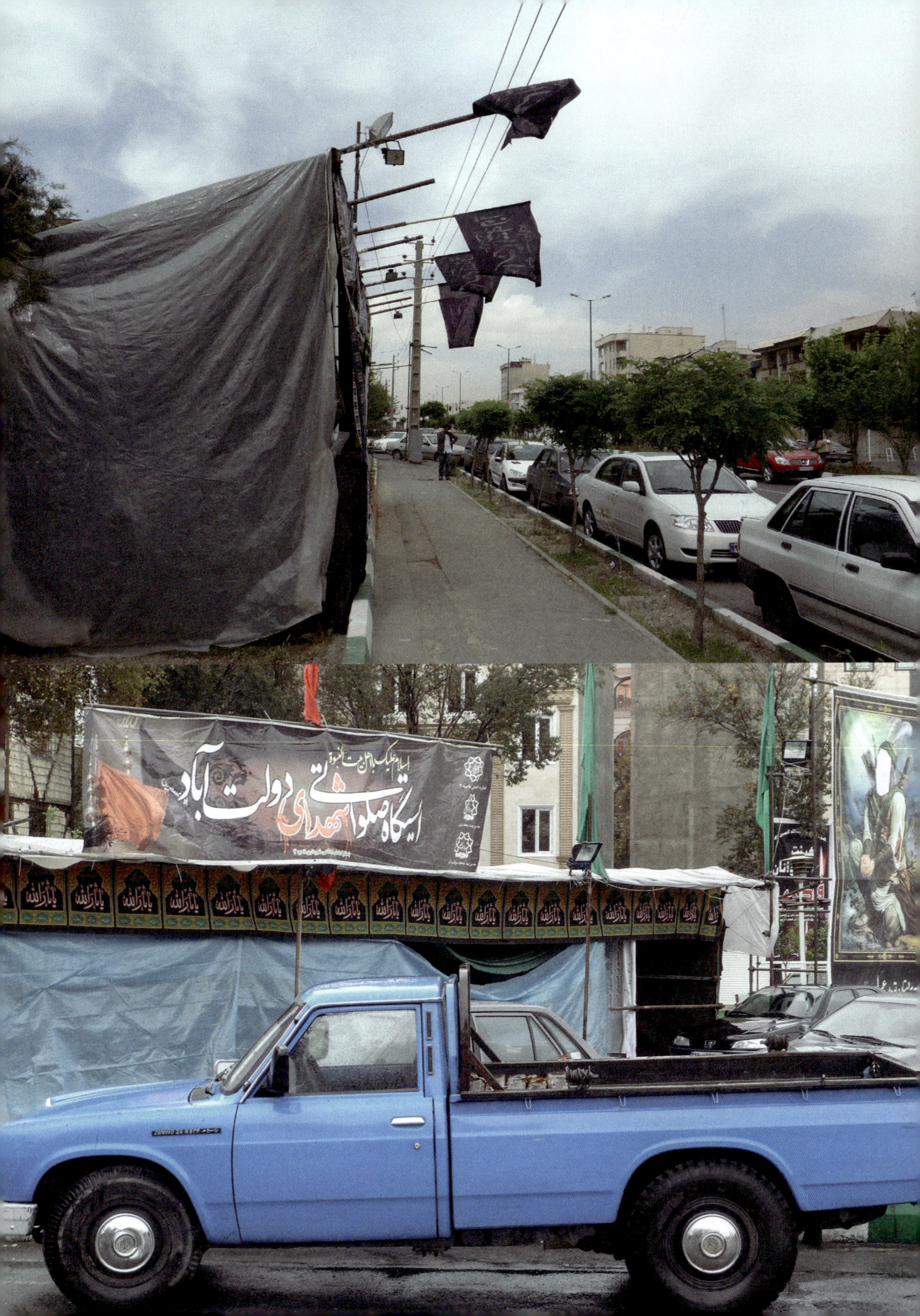
السلام علیک یا اهل بیت النبوة
ایستگاه صلواتی شهدای دولت آباد
یا ثارالله

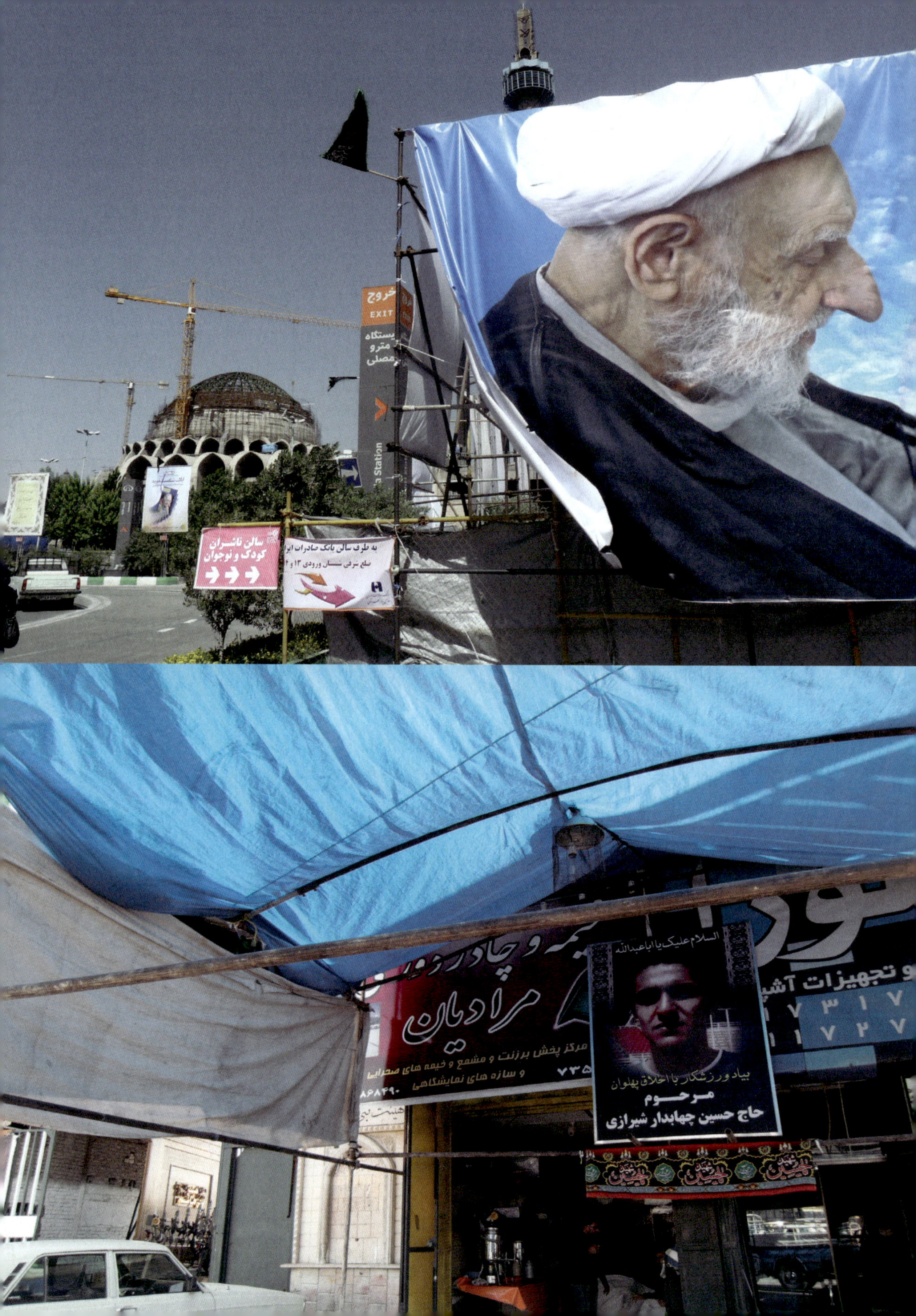

خروج
EXIT
یستگاه
مترو
مصلی
Station
سالن ناشران
کودک و نوجوان
به طرف سالن بانک صادرات ایر
ورودی ۱۳ و
مرادیان
مرکز پخش برزنت و مشمع و خیمه های صحرایی
و سازه های نمایشگاهی
و تجهیزات آش
السلام علیک یا اباعبدالله
بیاد ورزشکار با اخلاق پهلوان
مرحوم
حاج حسین چهابدار شیرازی

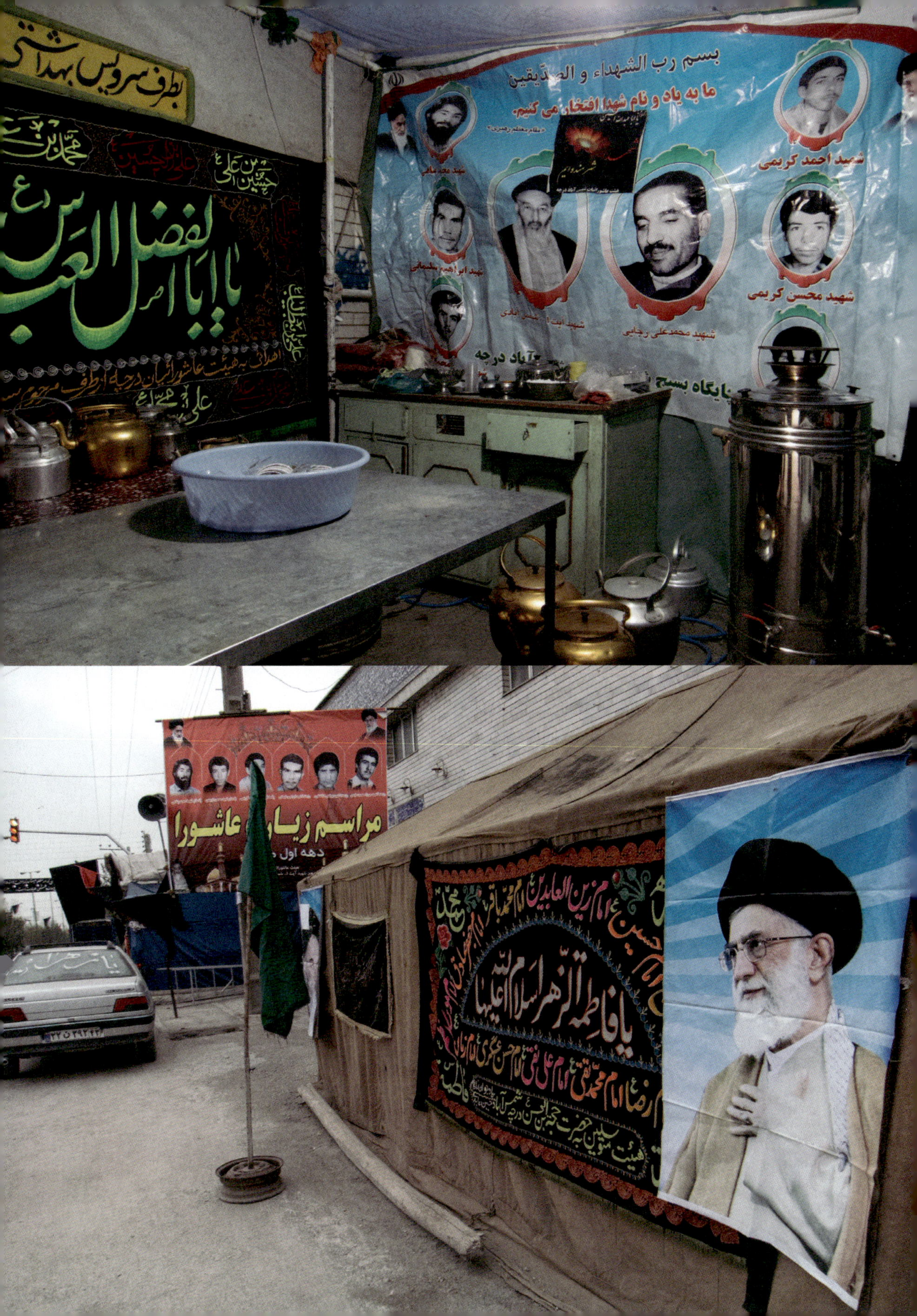

بطرف سرویس بهداشتی
بسم رب الشهداء و الصدّیقین
ما به یاد و نام شهدا افتخار می کنیم.
شهید احمد کریمی
شهید محسن کریمی
شهید محمدعلی رجایی

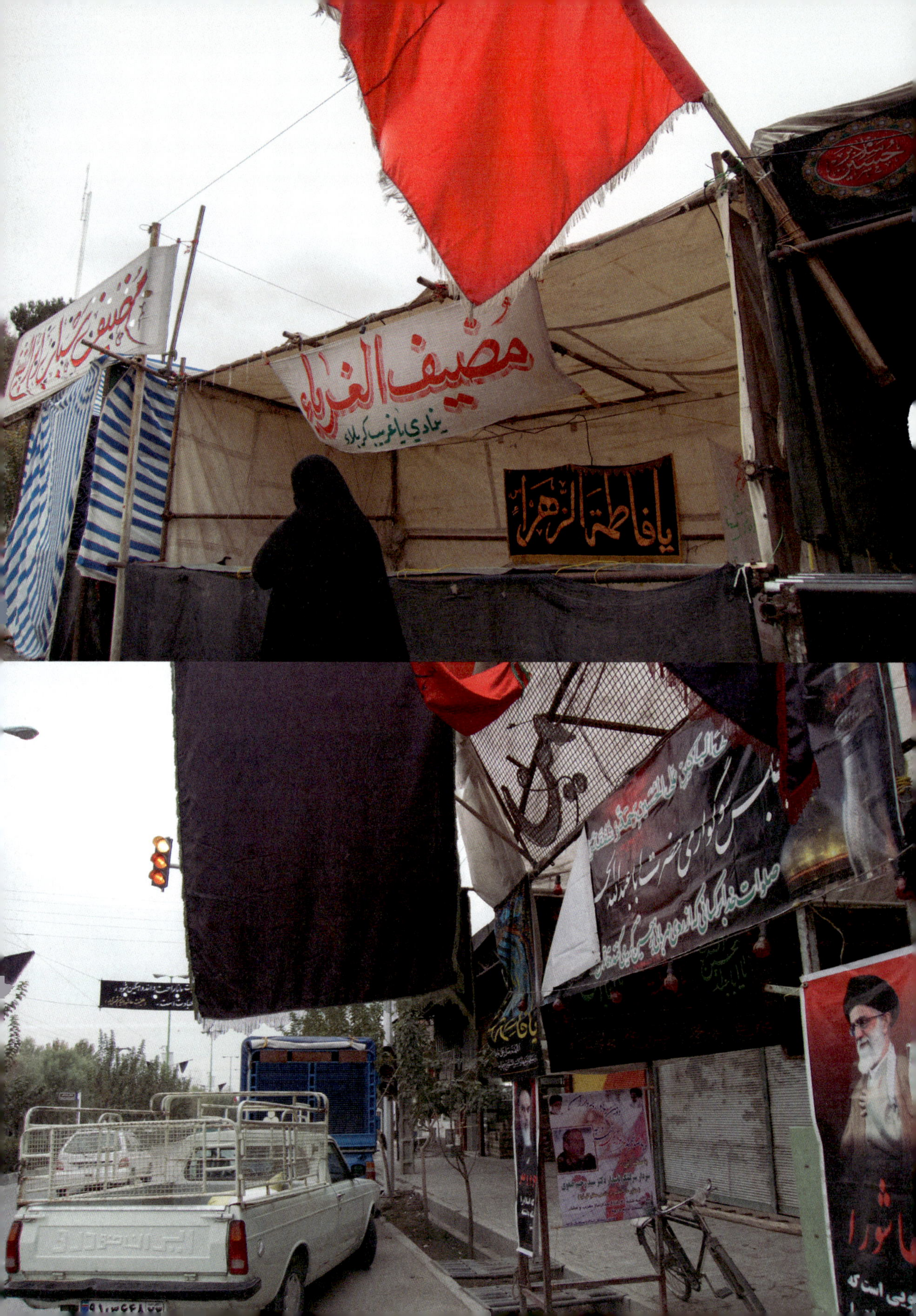
مضيف الغرباء
يا فاطمة الزهراء

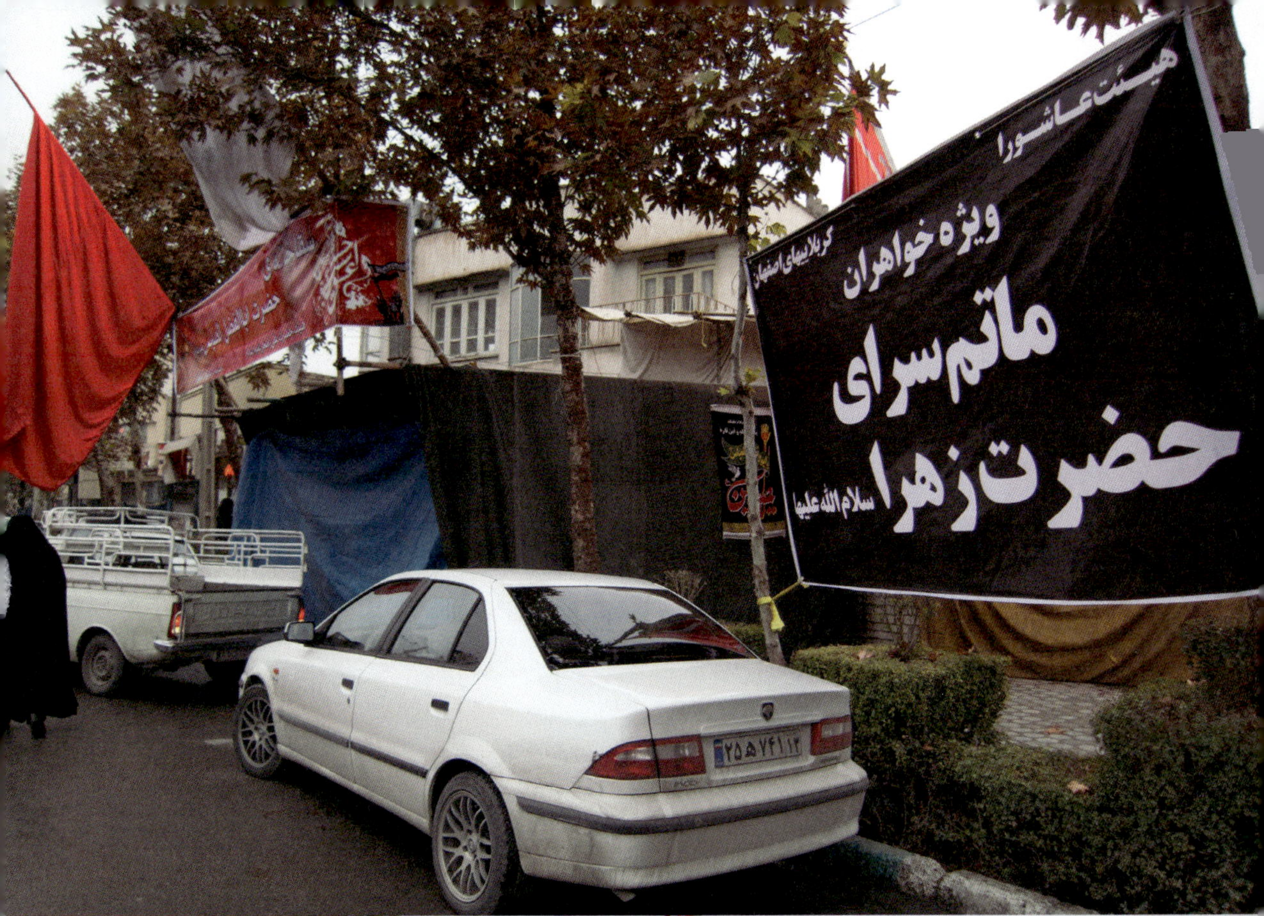

هیئت عاشورا
کربلاییهای اصفهان
ویژه خواهران
ماتم سرای
حضرت زهرا سلام الله علیها

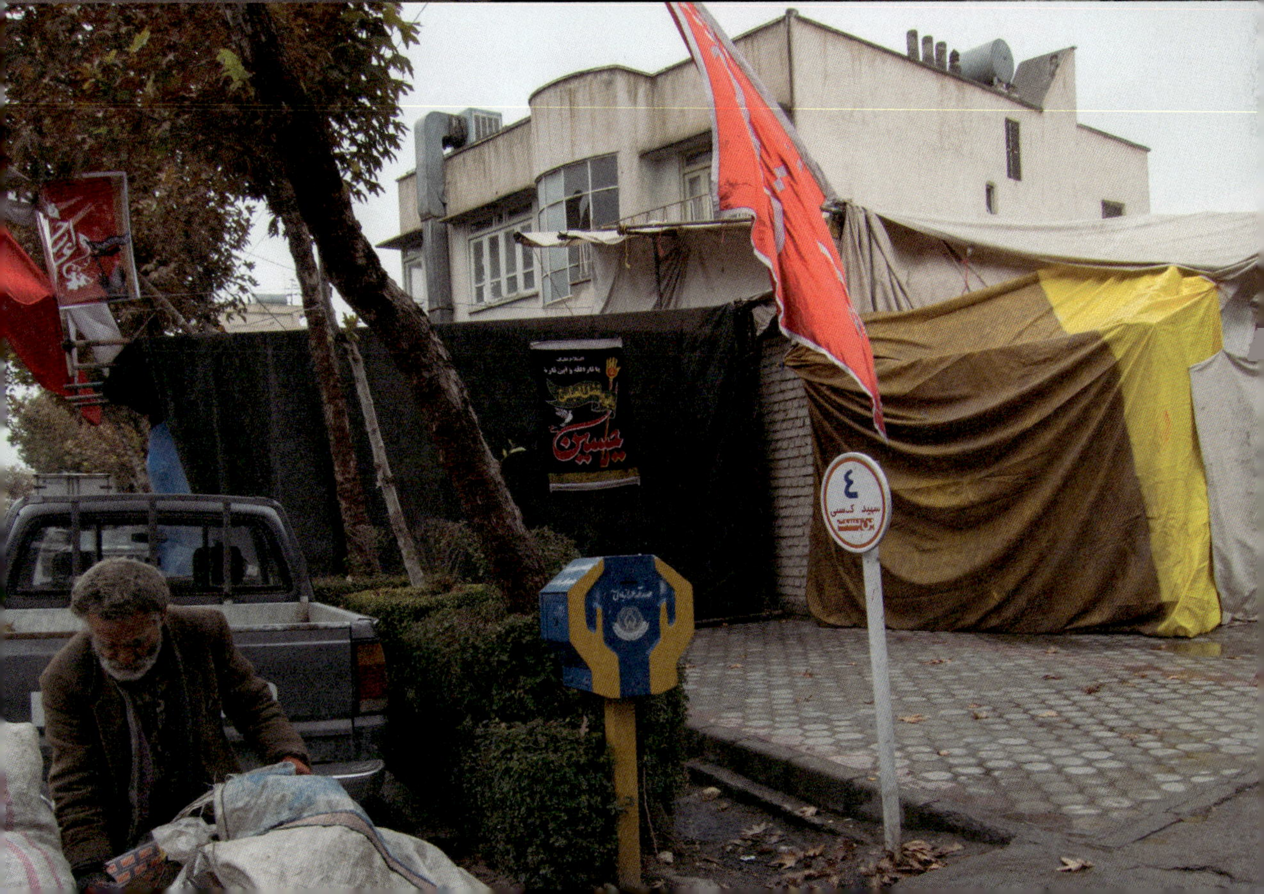

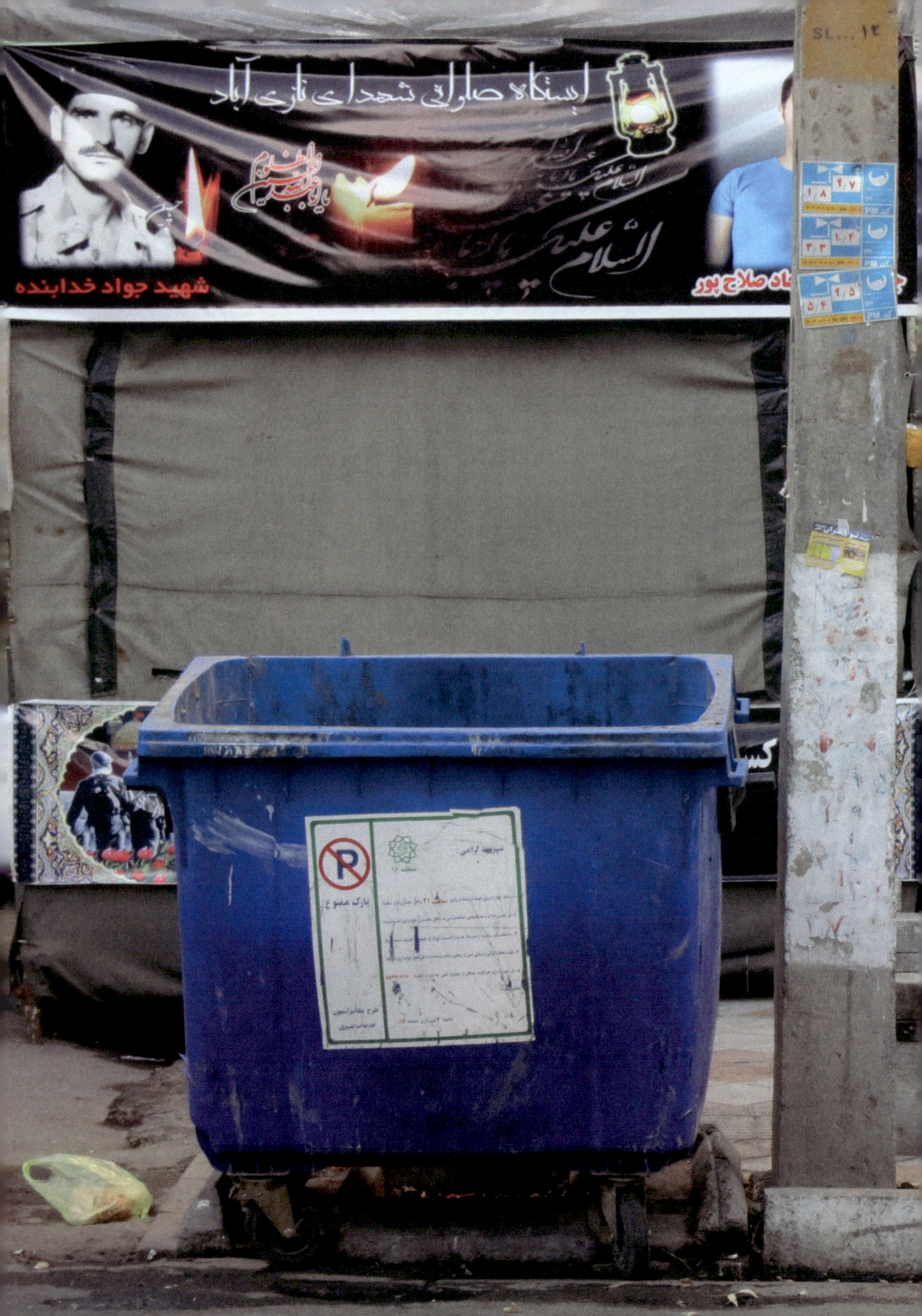

ایستگاه صلواتی شهدای نازی آباد
شهید جواد خدابنده
صلاح پور
پارک ممنوع

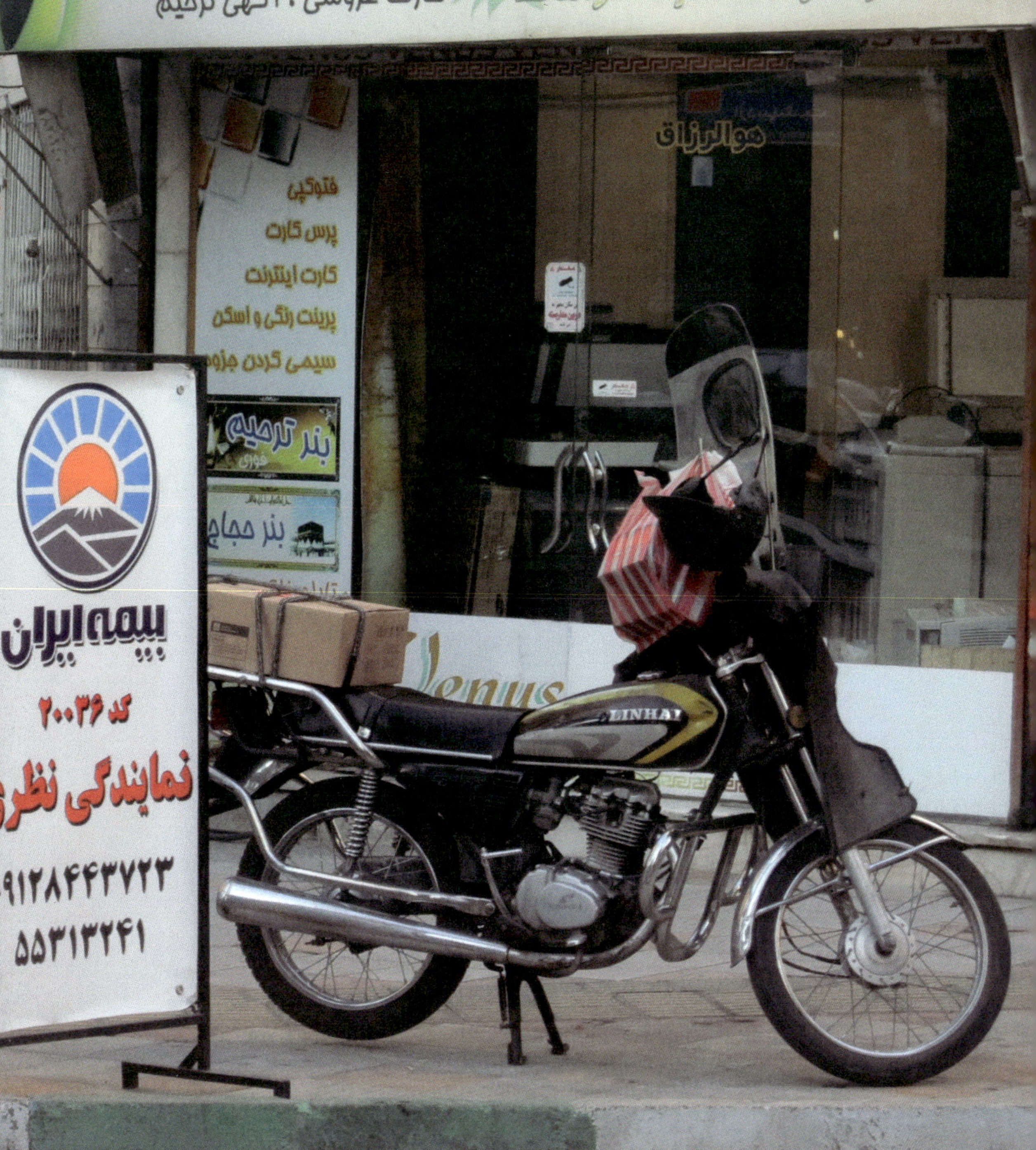

ونوس
Design & Printing & Publicize
جعبه ، کاتالوگ ، بروشور ، ست اداری
کارت ویزیت ، تراکت ، فاکتور ، پاکت
چاپ بنر و فلکسی ، استیکر
کارت عروسی ، آگهی ترحیم
هوالرزاق
فتوکپی
پرس کارت
کارت اینترنت
پرینت رنگی و اسکن
بنر ترحیم
فوری
LINHAI
بیمه ایران
کد ۲۰۰۳۶
۵۵۳۱۳۲۴۱

"What is looking at us?" and "Who is watching whom?" are questions that seem to have insinuated themselves into my life.
Before I left for Iran, I saw Castellucci's *The Minister's Black Veil.*[1] It has haunted me ever since.
The play is about a minister who decides to veil his face, day and night, for the rest of his life. This personal act of resistance is perceived as so inhuman by everyone in his village that he is expelled from the community. He has become a threat because he can no longer be controlled: the terrible veil has made objectification impossible. This fascinating piece ends with a stage crowded with convulsive "looking machines": looking at us, looking at each other, looking into the void.

Veils and curtains challenge the transparency that makes everything consumable and controllable. They install a reversed panopticism.[2]

The eye and its power: who is mastering whom?

1. Romeo Castellucci (Director) – Socìetas Raffaello Sanzio (Company), *The Minister's Black Veil* (free interpretation of the short story by Nathaniel Hawthorne)

2. Kristof van Baarle, *Language: Impossible* (Ghent University, Faculty of Arts and Philosophy, 2011)

"The perfect dictatorship would basically be a prison without walls in which prisoners would not even dream of escaping. It would essentially be a system of slavery where the slaves would love their servitude."

Attributed to Aldous Huxley

Huxley's statement "Man had built higher than he could climb" sets the tone of his *Brave New World:*[3] a perfectly organised society where everyone is happy. This happiness is owed to the free, sophisticated drug soma.
He sketches two main characters: John the Savage, an outsider who falls apart within the structures with which he can never reconcile himself and ends up committing suicide; and Bernard, who, despite being highly critical, resentful and sullen, refuses to take soma. The latter ends up isolated on an island with similar people in order to minimise his impact on the social order.

3. Aldous Huxley, *Brave New World* (Chatto & Windus, 1932)

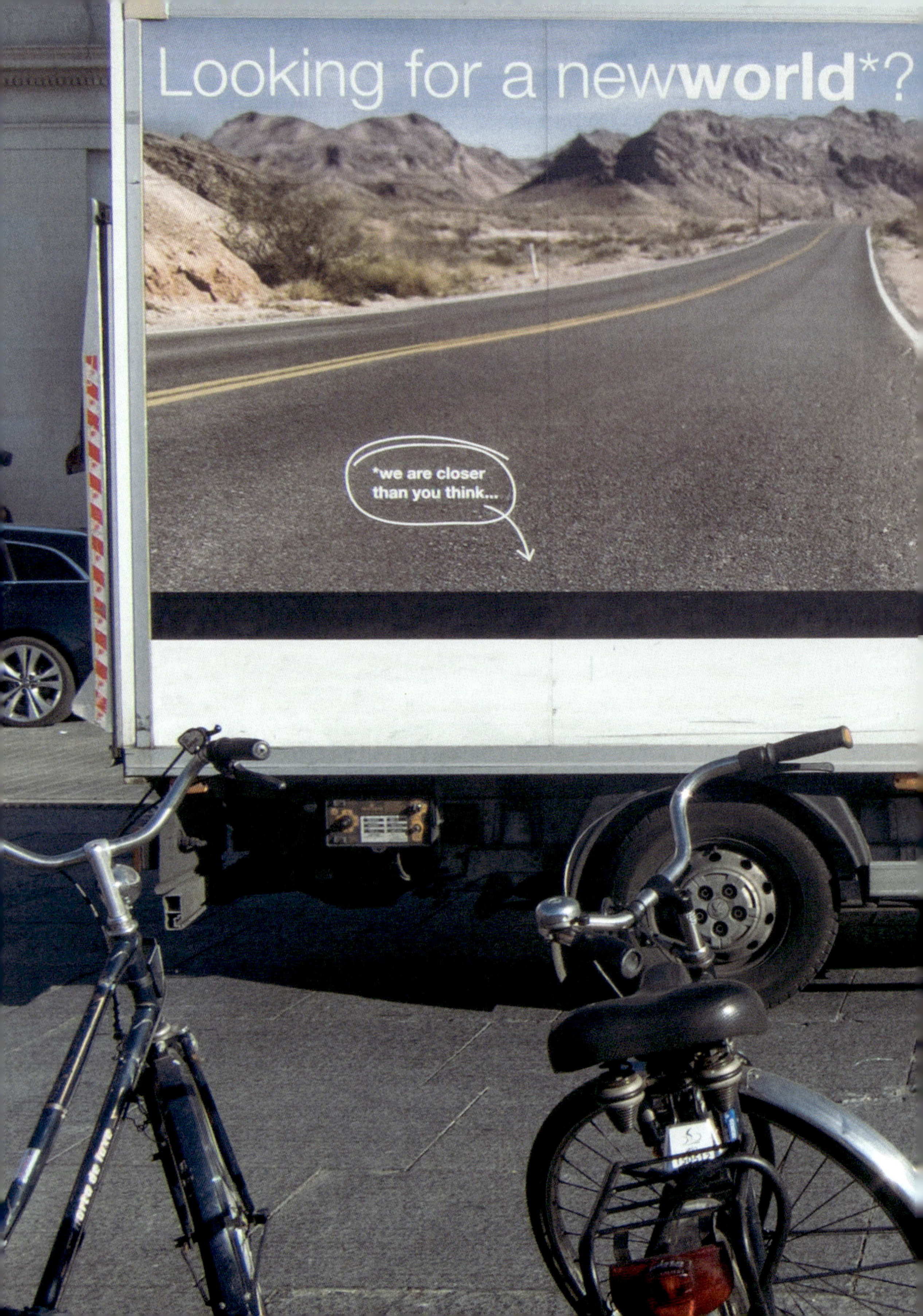
Looking for a newworld*?
*we are closer
than you think...

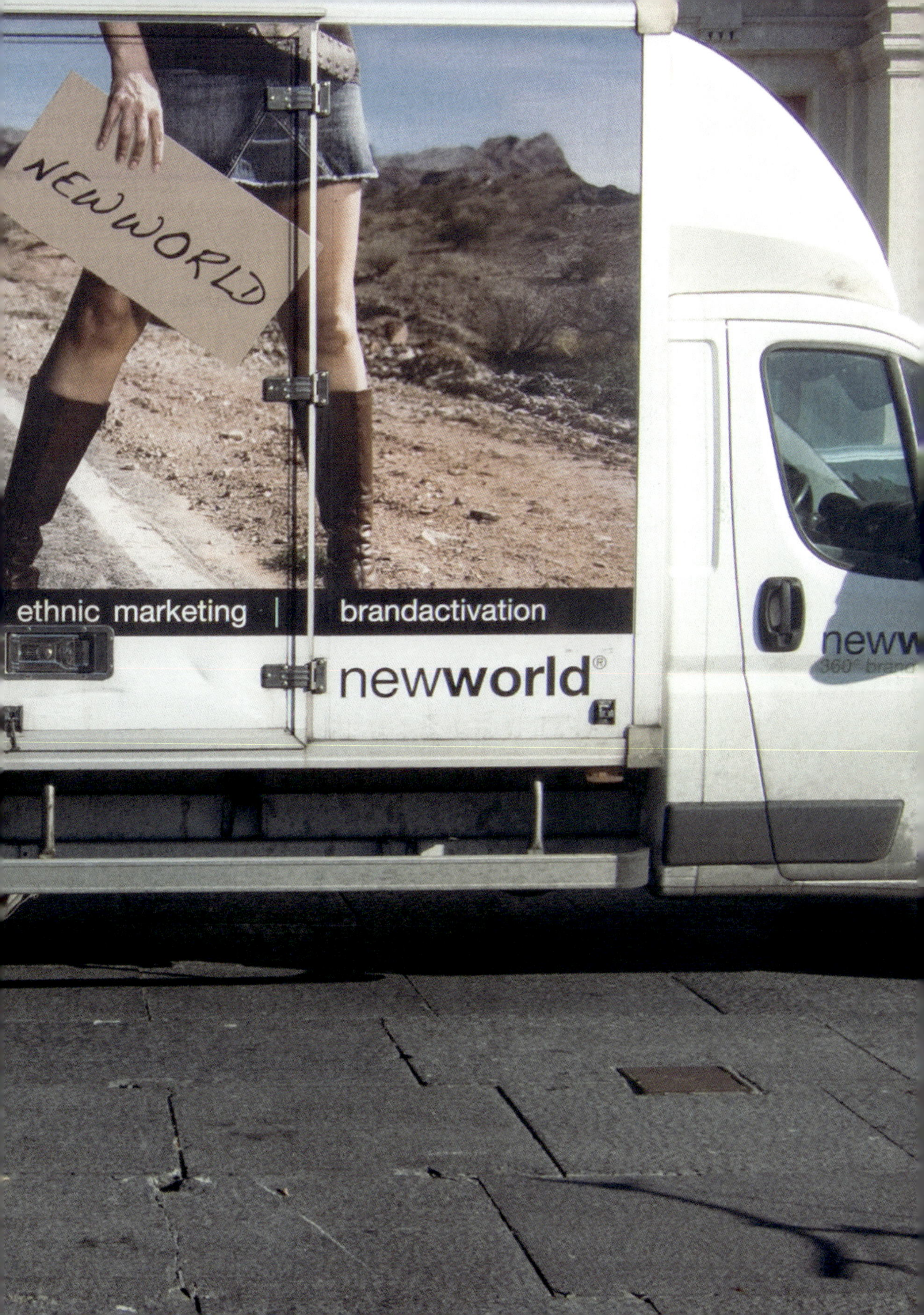
NEWWORLD
ethnic marketing | brandactivation
newworld®

INNER EXCLUSIONS

At home

In Iran, public and private spaces seem to be pervaded by a metaphysical all-seeing eye. This externalised eye is invested with authority. It is actually possible to negotiate with this gaze. The public space, on the other hand, is controlled by a political viewpoint that enforces a specific identity and eliminates anything that does not comply with it. This identity goes back centuries and is both religious and political in origin. The two perspectives seem to be ineluctably intertwined.
Public space is strict: the outdoors is public and the indoors is private.
Today, the "outside" is imbued with a past that is subject to continual updating.
The Ta'ziyeh is a phenomenon of daily life that contributes to this perpetual revisionism. Ta'ziyeh is a type of street theatre that creates a setting for social interactions. Ta'ziyeh performances provide a platform for coming together and function as the engine for a community populated by both religious and non-religious members. The Ta'ziyeh tents are a variety of sizes, thereby demarcating a space using the most rudimentary of means. They provide the infrastructure for a specific content. The aesthetic aspect of the tents is considered unimportant: they are simply inexpensive enclosures. They seem to be everywhere in the public space, apparently randomly and haphazardly erected on roadsides, squares and in alleys. Any empty space is a potential tent site. There are large versions for performances and small ones where tea and food is served. They carry a religio-political message and inject the past into the future but not in any transformed or associative way: it is literal and repetitive. This literalness demonstrates the static, non-transformative nature of the identity that the political agenda imposes. Here, the outdoors appears to be almost a dressed set. Indoors, on the other hand, seems to be a haven for personal fulfilment or, in the triumphant words of an Assyrian woman in Tehran with whom I stayed for a while: "Who I am and what I do at home is nobody's business!"

Note (1)

The blurred boundaries between outside and inside or visible and invisible have always interested me. The covert – or deliberately rendered invisible – guides and controls the visible.
Indoors can feel as though constantly subjected to a visual and mental dissection.
A façade is still only useful as a material barrier to weather events.
This impression of continual screening turns a personal cluster between 4 walls - far removed from any interference from the outside world - into a mental bankruptcy.
Actions seem at times to have been coordinated from an invisible realm. All borders dissolve in the process of instrumentalisation. The necessity to be able to be everything at all times is not limited to the indoors or the outdoors.
Transparency appears to be a precept.
The eye does not record or judge but penetrates everything and everyone. Who I am at home seems to be someone's business.

Ta'ziyeh plays are interpretations of a mythologised battle: the Battle of Kerbala, which took place in 680 AD. Following the death of Mohammed in 632, there was a dispute over who should be the new leader. This conflict would lead to the establishment of two groups that still exist to this day and which are now known as the Sunnis and Shiites. The followers of the caliphs would become the Sunnis, while the followers of the Imam would become the Shiites. On the 10th of October 680, when Imam Hussain ibn Ali was on his way to Kufa with 72 of his men, Caliph Yazied I's army cut him off at the pass. During the ensuing battle, Hussain ibn Ali and every single one of his men were killed.
The battle had political objectives: land and leadership. However, the processing of the defeat had a spiritual aspect that strongly informs the Shiite identity: opposition to what was perceived as unjust oppression. As with any mythical story, multiple readings are possible: a particular reading can be deliberately selected, exaggerated and staged in an opportunistic fashion.[4] This makes the myth an exceptional political tool that incites identification with the players.
The entire public sphere in Iran is dominated and controlled by an extensive and sophisticated network of images that reference this story. Unsurprisingly, a fair number of social movements have arisen that do not espouse this static, official frame of reference. For many, this results in a schizophrenic situation: social acceptance on an official level and social acceptance in the subgroup. Public and private are two different scenarios. If identification with the official is impossible, then as soon as the physical threshold is crossed to the outside world, self-preservation leads to self-correction and self-censorship. People put on a disguise. Each space proclaims the codes of conduct loud and clear.
It could be argued that such a rigid structure also provides a sense of security. One can follow the rules without personally engaging with them. The public space as a whole can be perceived as a theatre in which the polar opposites of identification and detachment are both present.

4. Janet Afary & Kevin B. Anderson, *Foucault and the Iranian Revolution: Gender and the Seductions of Islamism* (University of Chicago Press, 2005)

Note (2)

During an interview with a practicing believer in Antwerp, the question was shyly asked, "and what is your religion? Or is that too personal a question?" It was as though they felt like they were peeking into someone's bedroom.
This gave me a strange, paradoxical feeling. The two extremes of intimacy and transparency often seem to coincide, I believe, and not so much from personal intention as from outside interference. This leads to the uncomfortable sensation of not being able to keep the outside world out. Distance is thereby erased and the outside becomes personal while the inside becomes impersonal. The theatre is inverted.
In this context, is the perception of a religion even possible beyond the perception of its media value? Or for a person's self-perception to differ from the way the self is presented?

The gaze is not authoritarian but devious; it seems to be trying to extract something.
Both indoors and outdoors feel like a massive arena for exhibitionism, where everyone fights for their own uncertain identity while, when it comes to religion, that of the neighbour can only be tolerated by dismissing it as nonsense.[5]
I ask myself where the space is for the hidden to be itself: places where identities are no one else's business and cannot be appropriated by anyone but the owner and their imaginary other. What physical places could manifest these backrooms of the mind? In what blind corner can people find shelter?
At an exhibition in Tehran, I saw a painting that contained two images: the one that was visible concealed the "real" image behind hatches. This represents one way of evading censorship. Interestingly, the painting directly paralleled the actual space: the "official" exhibition was on display in the front room and the "real" exhibition in the back room. Hidden rooms are meaningful and have an impact on both a practical and a psychological level.

5. Donald Loose, "It takes two to tango", in: Donald Loose & Anton de Wit (eds.), *Religie in het publieke domein. Fundament en fundamentalisme,* p. 10 (Damon, 2007)

The Ta'ziyeh is a form of passion play that aims to blur the boundaries between the current actuality and the imaginary past. The body is an archaic form of memory conduit. But rather than a memory storage system that creates of the past an autonomous entity, this memory system does not access dead pathways or objects that have been registered, catalogued and stored. Instead it is a physical performance of the past that is staged over and over and over again. During the ceremonial re-enactments of this shared memory, there is hardly any distinction made between the actors and the public. They become interchangeable since everyone contributes to bringing the myth to life. Spectators may project their own private tragedies on to the larger screen of the epic tale of heroism – one with a higher objective than the strictly personal.[6]
There are several traits inherent to the Ta'ziyeh that promote its political instrumentalisation, among which are its power to bind people together and the access it provides to a mass audience. A more nationalistic concept can easily be selected. This has repeatedly occurred: for example, during the Iranian Revolution of 1979 and during the Iran-Iraq war that followed. The results of the first event and the traumas of the second are still being processed by Iranian society. The Ta'ziyeh served as a recruitment machine. Ta'ziyeh performances and Mourning Ceremonies are attended by huge crowds and are a part of the street life for at least 3 months of the year. This massive popularity and visibility makes it into a mass medium suitable for disseminating political messages.
The side effect is that it automatically creates exclusivity. Many were condemned to homelessness. Bonds were broken due to different religious persuasions or a lack

of religious conviction. The casual tent constructions, which aurally blend the inside and outside through their thin membranes, establish a single identity. The public space becomes utterly homogenous.
A binary system of authorisation and creeping prohibition produces actual expulsions: people are pushed “out”. This psychologically unsafe outdoor space encompasses everything, including interiors.

6. Janet Afary & Kevin B. Anderson, *Foucault and the Iranian Revolution: Gender and the Seductions of Islamism* (University of Chicago Press, 2005)

Note (3)

The creation of a common enemy is a classic feature of all forms of repression. Demonisation is constantly there, lurking in the shadows, waiting to rear its ugly head when a sovereign power feels at its most vulnerable.
The discourse in which I constantly seem to find myself - about the all-inclusive space that makes claims on universal truths - can only exist by establishing antithetical hierarchies in space and time. The demarcation lines are frequently contested, both there and here, and are dependant on both the position that is taken and the power mechanism that is considered acceptable, or, conversely, inconceivable. I believe that it is easier to fight a power that has a clear, concrete face than one that hides in an all-absorbent atmosphere that makes it impossible to know what or with whom one is fighting, let alone how to go about it. Resistance, in no matter what form, will then ricochet off an invisible wall of immunity, just as the drug soma in Huxley’s *Brave New World* – non-toxic and freely available – created a paralysing acceptance in the people.
Political forms of censorship seem to manifest themselves violently; economic forms of censorship are silent as they are not imposed through prohibitions but instead through numerical mechanisms.[7]
Paranoia is a product of both: each produces imaginary enemies who wish to undermine the installed ideology.
I came across an installation, *Silent Space,* at an art fair in Berlin. This space provided an oasis of mental freedom; the emptiness had infinite possibilities and once outside again, the unequivocality of the contrast was breath-taking. Freedom in the form of endless options was replaced by a claustrophobic tunnel in which every opening was strategically closed. The silent space became a ghost of itself. It was swallowed up by a compulsive monoculture. It lost its boundless openness in which each identity is obliged to define itself over and over again due to the lack of boundaries. It dissolves as soon as it becomes exclusive rather than inclusive.

7. Geert Beulens e.a. (ed.) *De militanten van de limiet. Over censuur en vrije meningsuiting* (Van Halewijck, 2000)

The Shia identity was politically mobilised during the Iranian Revolution. The fluid, more hybrid and layered aspects of this identity and its interpretations hardened to form a simple militant front. At the time, the revolution was applauded by the French philosopher Michel Foucault, who as a journalist ended up in Tehran. He was asked by the leading Italian newspaper Corriere della Sera to be a special correspondent reporting on the Iranian Revolution. He went to Iran in order to witness what he called "the birth of ideas" and the emergence of "spiritual politics".
Foucault wanted to gain inspiration from this revolution for ways to escape the grip of a cerebral, modern society that he had long criticised, with its ideology of the quantifiable, manageable and manipulable person. He hailed the revolution as a potential challenger to disciplinary modernism.
With his leaning towards Oriental cultures, he was a supporter of the Islamists who sought to break away from the culture and politics of the modernist regime of the Shah. The Islamists also criticised a purely materialistic view of life.
The dualist positioning of nostalgic orientalism, which is informed by a preference for archaic social structures, and cold rational modernism was subsequently heavily criticised. This period was painstakingly covered. The failure of the revolution was an anti-climax for many.[8] As Altoussa H. responded to Foucault in 1978: "The Western left should not let itself be seduced by a cure that is perhaps worse than the disease".[9]
The concept of spiritual politics is very alluring: a type of politics that issues from the very fibre of social relations and ways of life.

8. Janet Afary & Kevin B. Anderson, *Foucault and the Iranian Revolution: Gender and the Seductions of Islamism* (University of Chicago Press, 2005)

9. Janet Afary & Kevin B. Anderson, *Foucault and the Iranian Revolution: Gender and the Seductions of Islamism* (University of Chicago Press, 2005)

Note (4)

My many trips to Turkey and then Iran aroused my interest in family ties and their implications in social cohesion. Family communes are firmly rooted in these countries. I caught myself feeling nostalgic, a sentiment that almost imperceptibly introduces another element: a gap in time.
In earlier attempts to unravel my own identity, I followed the trail of what I ultimately externalised as an "other". These traces of myself brought me to the anonymity of a collective past in my own country and finally into a theocracy. However, neither a temporal nor a geographical distance can rely on stable borders. Autonomy rapidly dissolves into an amalgam of associations. By let-

ting go of a linear, narrative concept of time, autonomy loses its core.
In an open field, the associations that emerge are by definition equal. This multifarious material, lacking linear reference points, provides a slippery, porous and hybrid field to which it is hard to attach new patterns and where existing patterns lose ground. Both exoticism and supremacy fail to catch on.
The territory that can exist between countries with their own separate authorities, whether God or the Quantifiable, is a territory without the need for guards. The power structures established by authorities produce their own outsiders in the same way that the ego creates an "other".
Nor is it the autonomous image, the demarcated cotainer, that lends meaning but rather the imagelessness in between.
In the mental fusion realm, far from the pragmatism of divisions and the dualistic "position" versus "opposition", each association presents itself as a new opportunity for meaning. This area is all-inclusive.

Foucault's fascination for the East and particularly for the revolution can be ascribed to his distaste for technological and verbal cultures. His appraisal of the Iranian Revolution was sharply criticised. The spiritual power of group contrition in which the individual disappears was so attractive to him that it had clouded his ability to see the political consequences. The participants of the revolution were actors in a giant Ta'ziyeh: they crawled into the skins of Imam Hussain's men who, centuries before, had refused to surrender out of loyalty even if that meant death - and did the same.[10]
Foucault admired the spirituality of those who were not afraid to face death and had no interest in those who would not join them.
The legacy of this radical and symbolic attitude to death is older than the Battle of Kerbala. Imam Hussain had a predecessor, Shiavus, whose death was also a symbolic indictment of injustice.[11]
Islamic Iran has a history that has been pushed into the background by the current government. This pre-Islamic legacy is mainly celebrated by West-leaning individuals. To them, the pre-Islamic era is the real and original Iran. For those affiliated to the Islamic regime, this period is considered a fabrication. While Shah Pahlavi ruled, Ta'ziyeh performances were banished from the cities, resulting in their status changing to that of a marginal phenomenon. Just before the Iranian Revolution, Shah Pahlavi put on a megalomaniac display of Persian history during a lavish banquet. On the occasion of the 2,500th anniversary of the Persian Empire, a "Golden City" (or "Tent City") was erected near the archaeological site of Persepolis and representatives of many countries were invited to partake in the festivities. The Golden City consisted of ingeniously designed tent structures and was intended to evoke a spurious connection between Shah Palavhi and Cyrus the Great. This diplomatic showcase – against the archaeological backdrop of Persepolis – included a costumed procession that staged the reclaimed history of the pre-Islamic Persian Empire. Heroics were projected on to an arid landscape studded with actual artefacts. This form of theatre was far removed from that of the Ta'ziyeh: purely patriotic in approach and utterly lacking in a spiritual element. No secret was made of these festivities, including the unfettered spending and the bias towards the West, and the event ultimately

contained the seeds of the revolution.
The iron skeletons of the tents were used by the military after the conflict ended and the site became, in its turn, an indictment of the Shah.[12]

10. Janet Afary & Kevin B. Anderson, *Foucault and the Iranian Revolution: Gender and the Seductions of Islamism* (University of Chicago Press, 2005)

11. Khosrow Shahriari, Breaking Down Borders and Bridging Barriers: Iranian Taziyeh Theatre (University of South Wales, 2006)

Note (5)

Before I went to Iran, I searched my own part of the world for places that might reveal something about my personal identity. I was examining the past in order to position myself in the present. Locations were chosen based on their historical contexts. In many cases, consciously or unconsciously, they were marginalised places. Looking at a barren piece of land with few visible vestiges of the past, I was struck by the absurdity of the enterprise. A glass wall appeared between the abandoned plot and myself. A floor became a screen for projections and was objectified as an area that had been placed outside of our time. Buildings and landscapes became mummified reference points. Stone and soil acted as containers for mental projections of practicable stories full of hiatuses and highlights. In the end, it doesn't matter what events they represent, what makes them historically relevant, but instead why they have been staged the way they have and at what point a building or landscape has been frozen in time to serve as a platform for ideological legitimacy.
The past that is represented dissolves when there is a thorough and intensive mental deconstruction. It can only manifest itself in the present when there are links between visual impressions and the available information. Traces of the past realign themselves over and over again to suit their new function: a dynamic in which neither the past nor the future is relevant. Images, sounds, texts and impressions weave in and out of each other in the here and now. They present themselves in situ.
Any identity is only continuously and immediately creative within this tissue of interlinked phenomena.

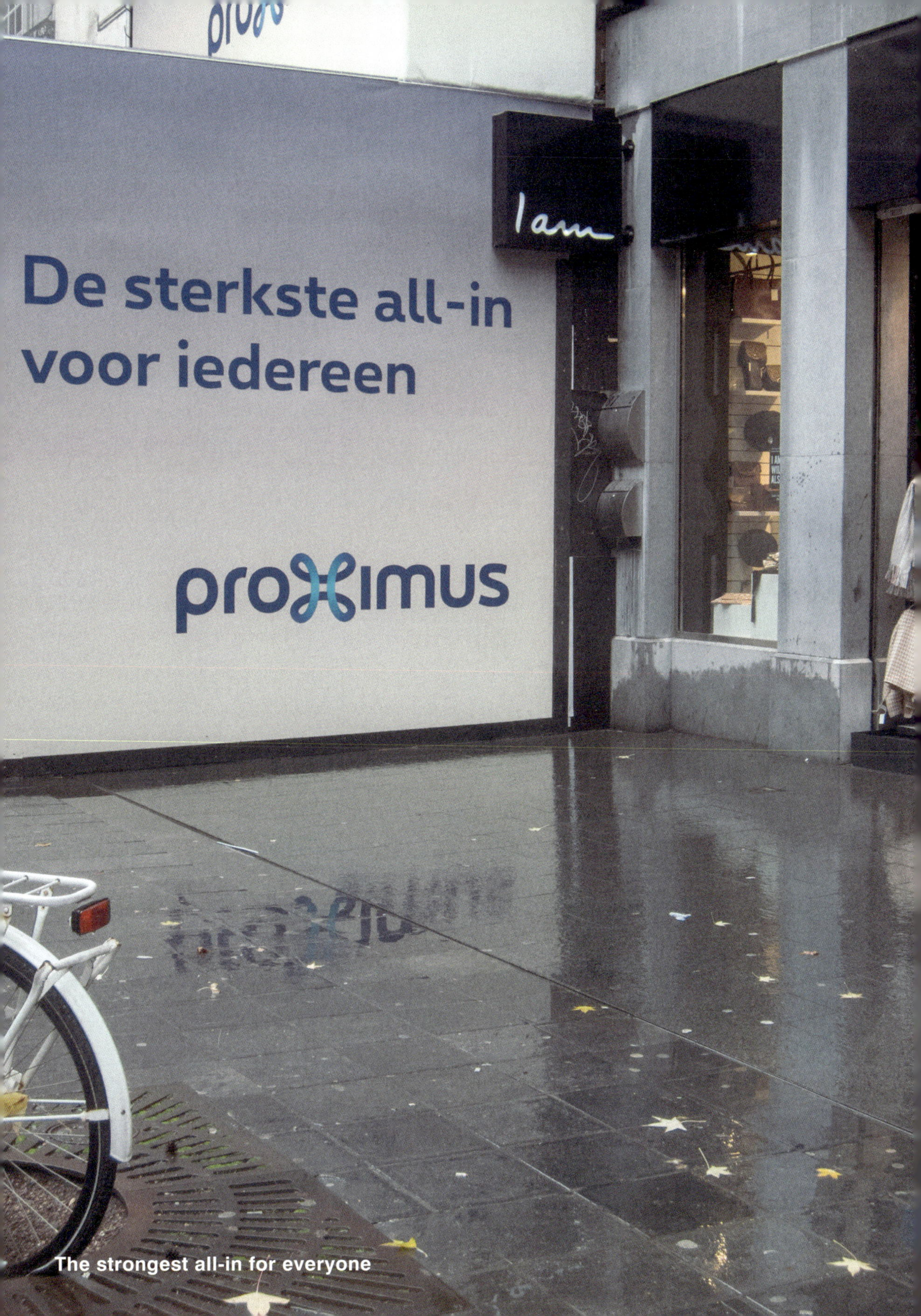

The strongest all-in for everyone

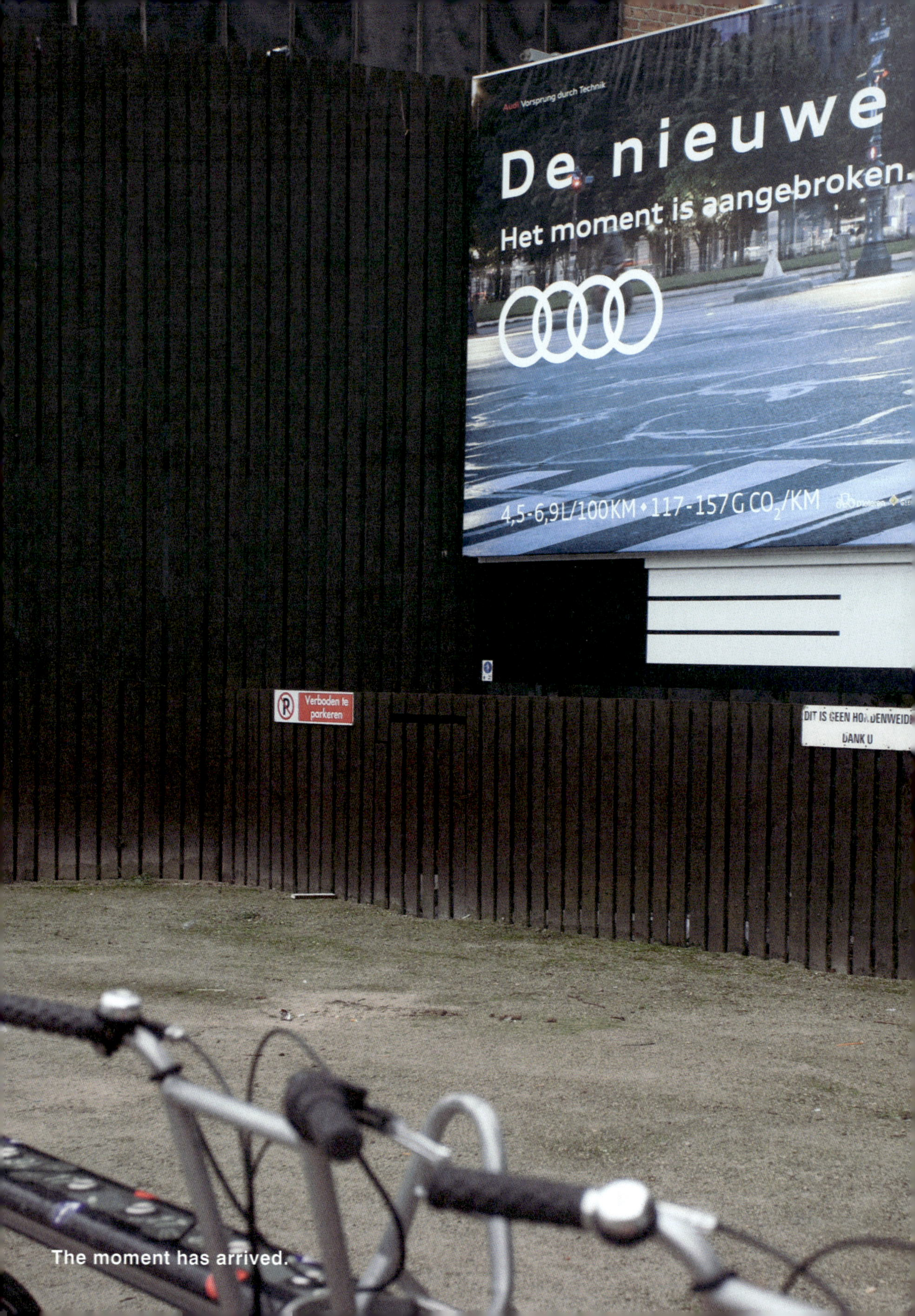

The moment has arrived.

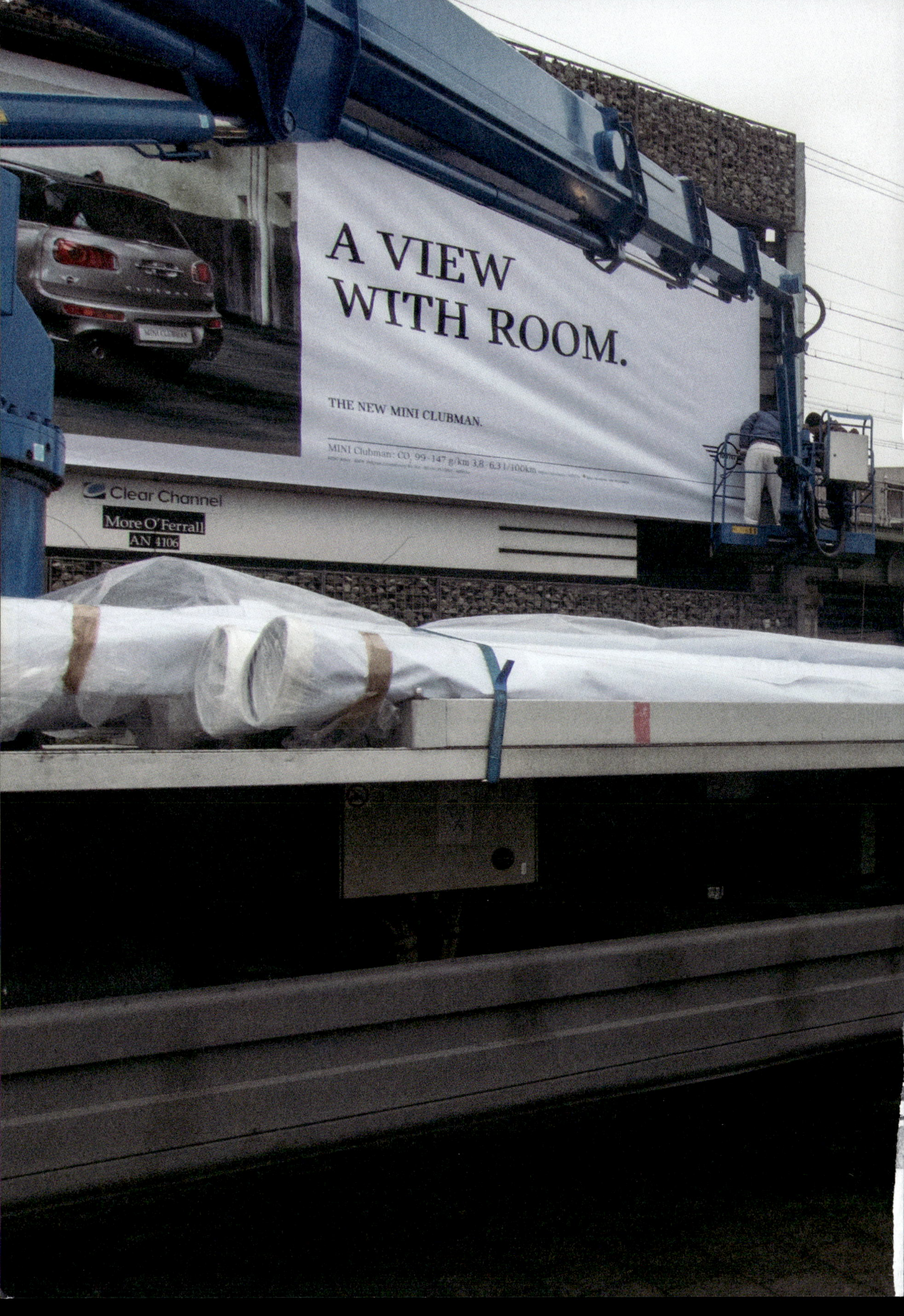
A VIEW
WITH ROOM.
THE NEW MINI CLUBMAN.
Clear Channel
More O'Ferrall
AN 4106

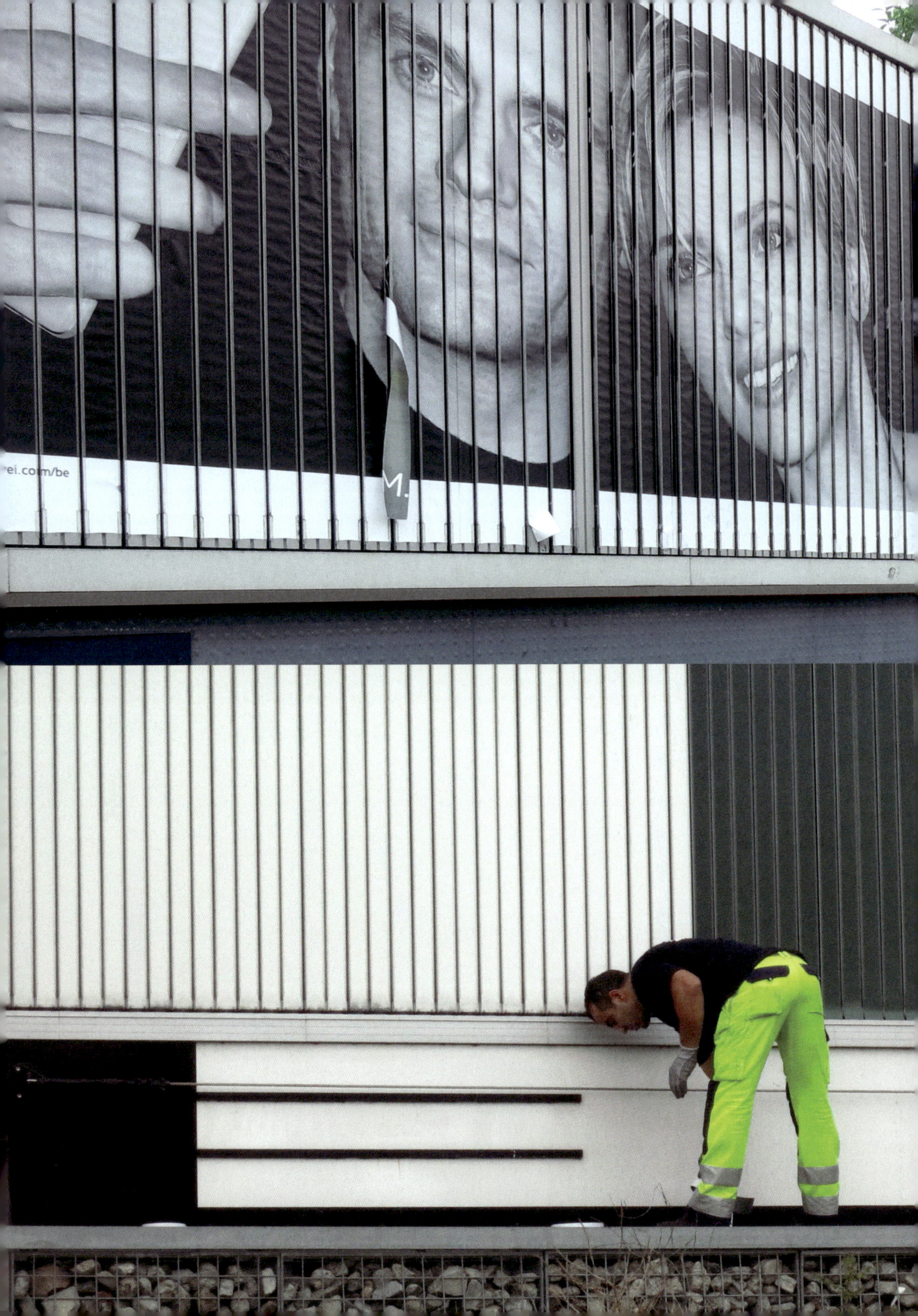
ei.com/be
M.

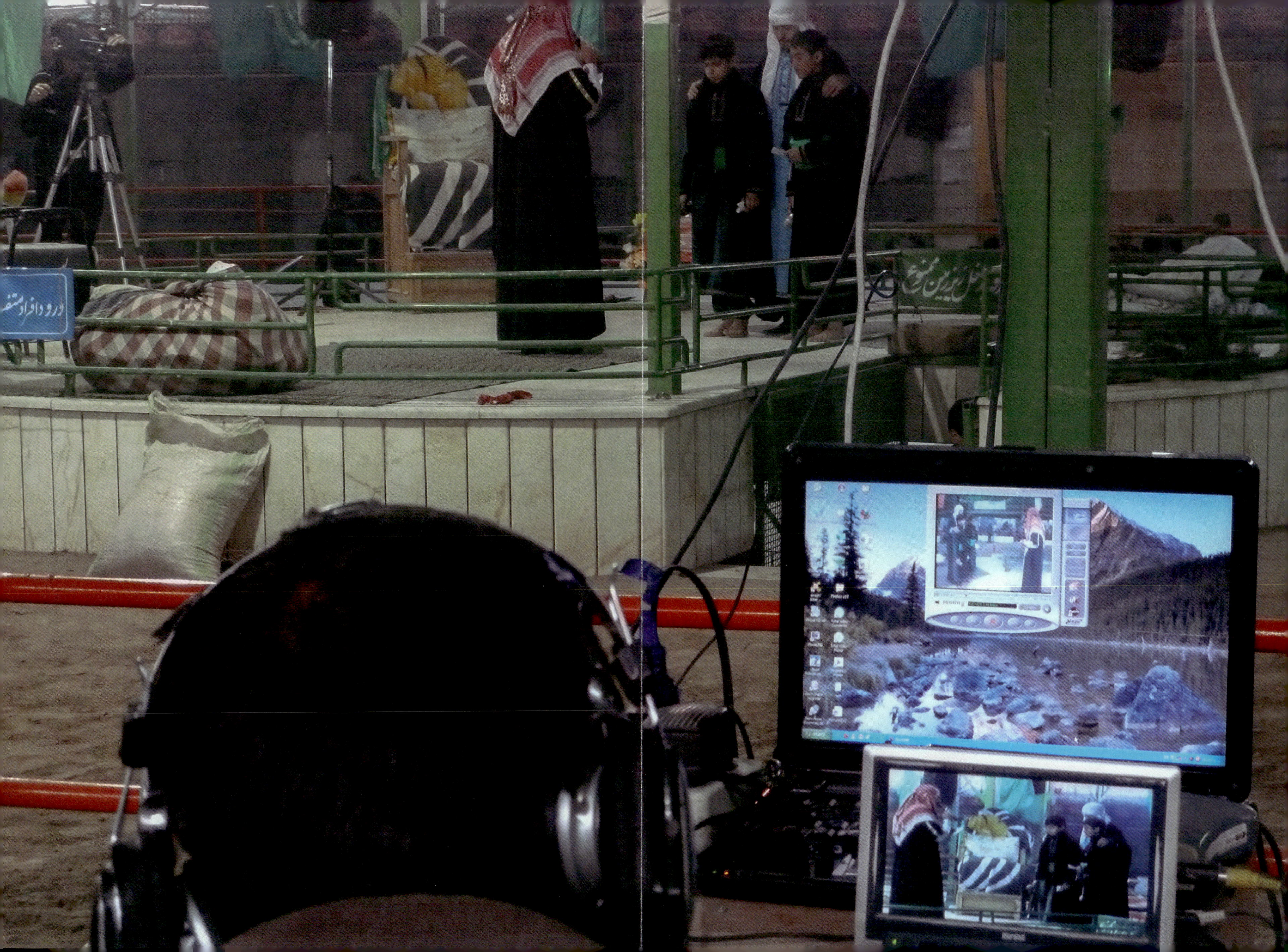
ورود افراد

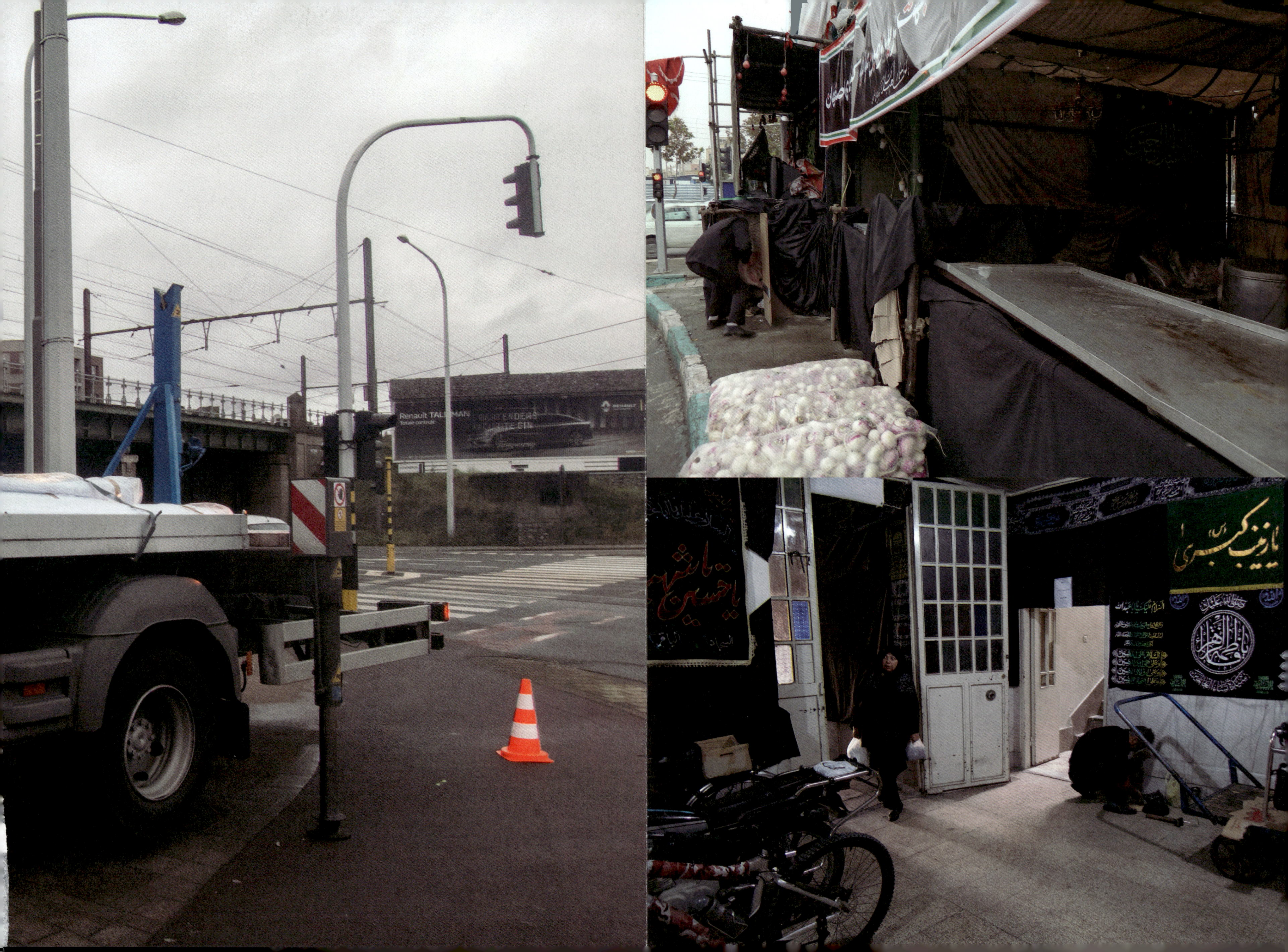
یا زینب کبری

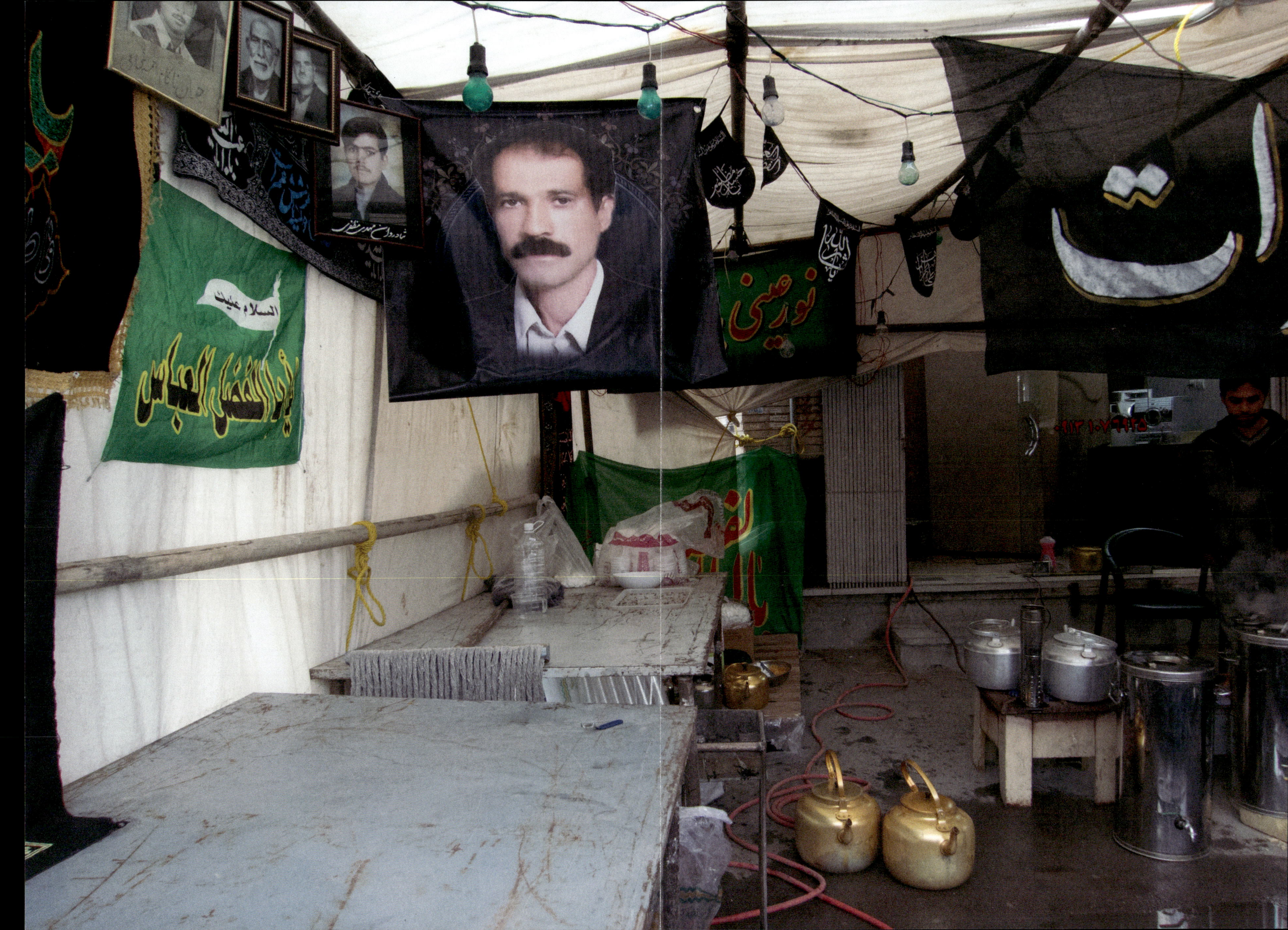

السلام علیک
یا ابا الفضل العباس
نور عینی

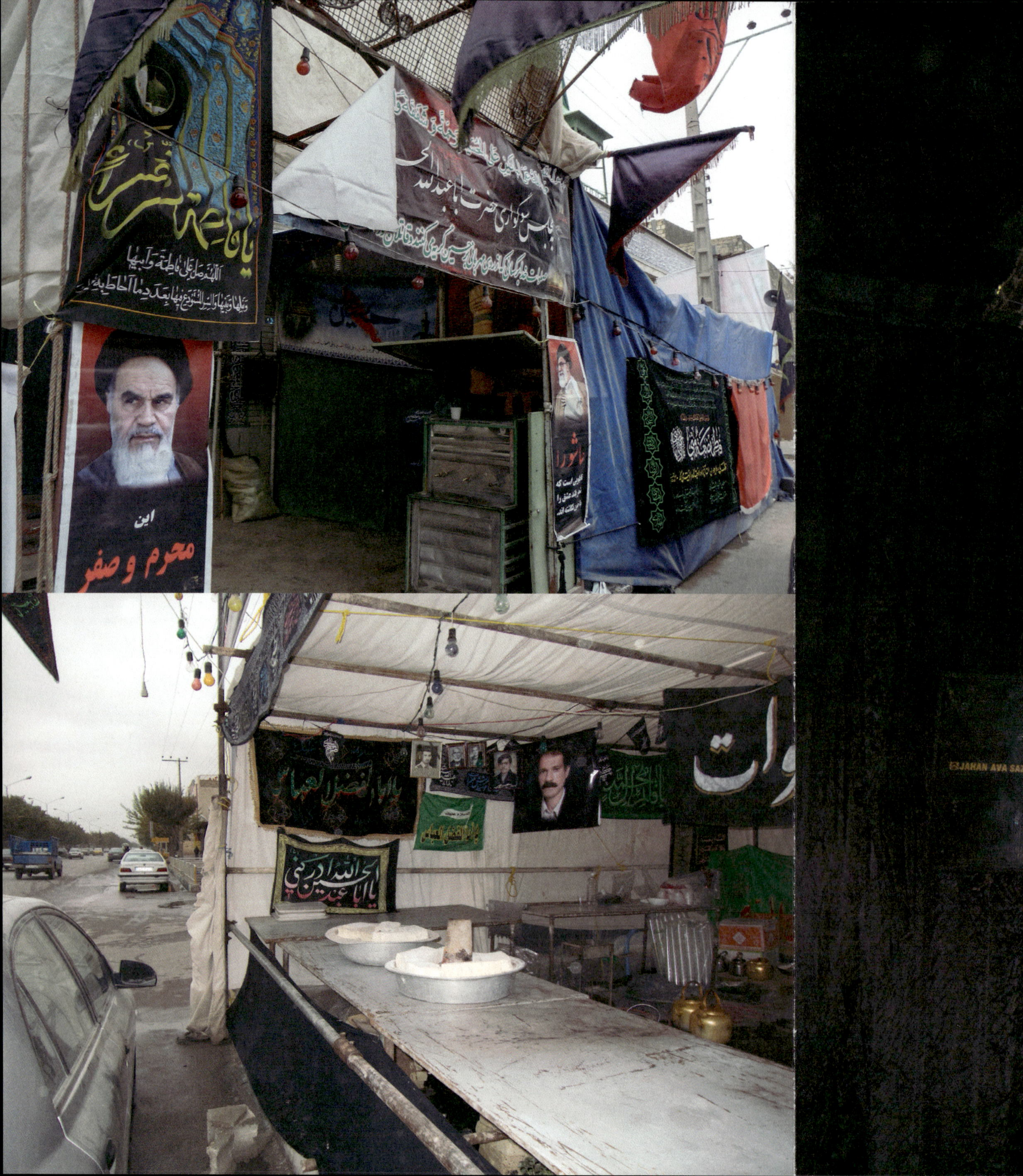
این
محرم و صفر

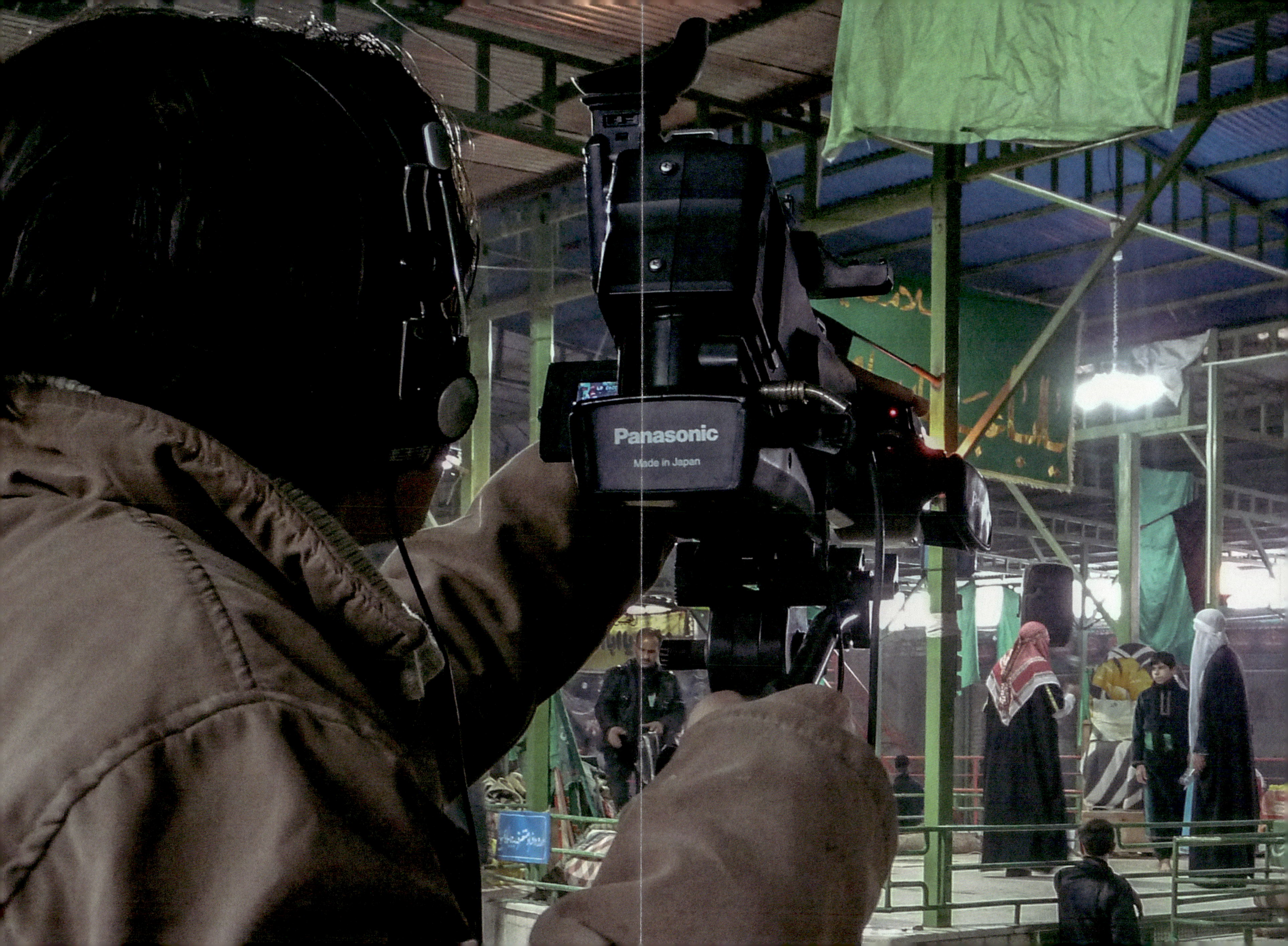
Panasonic
Made in Japan

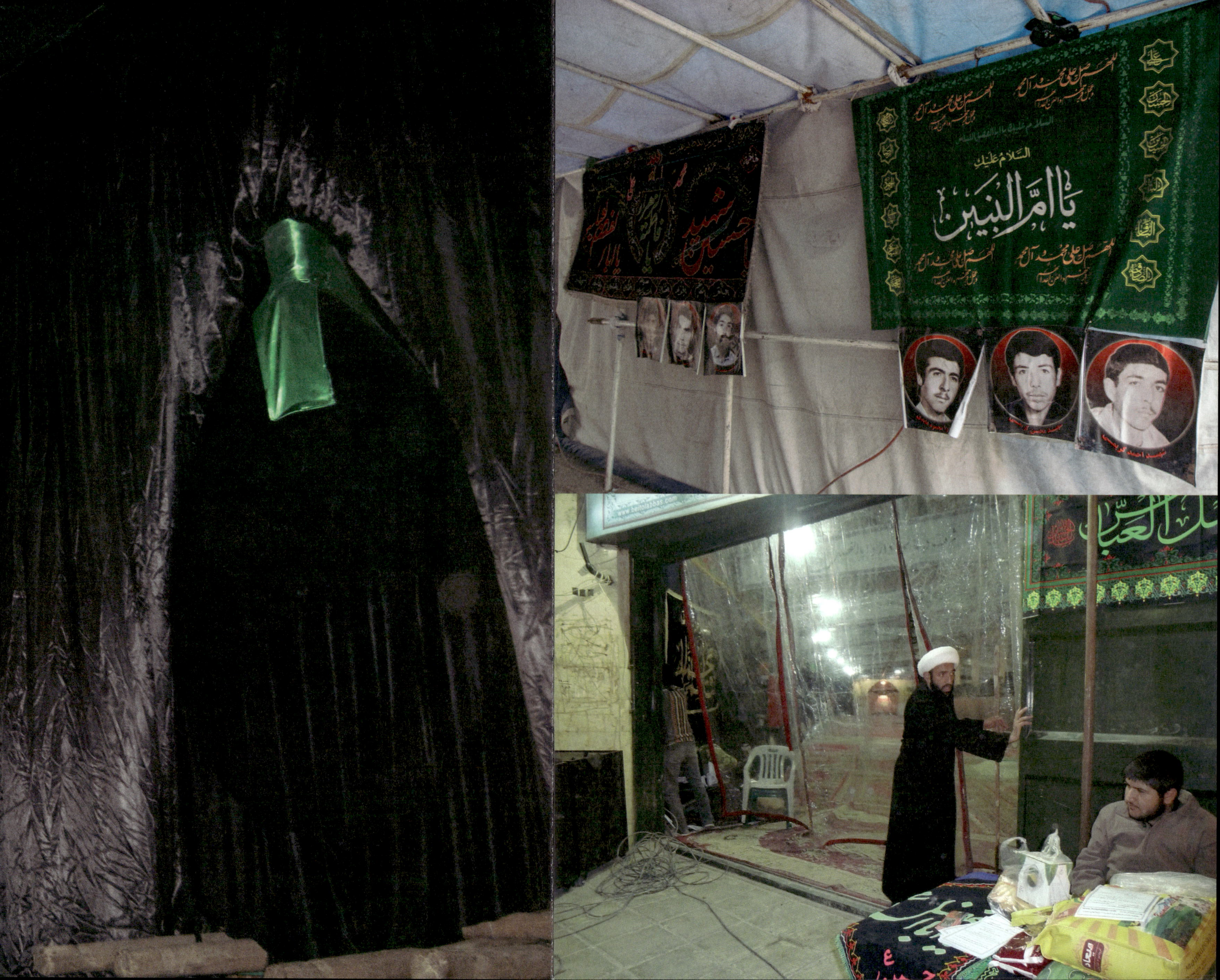
السلام علیک
یا ام البنین

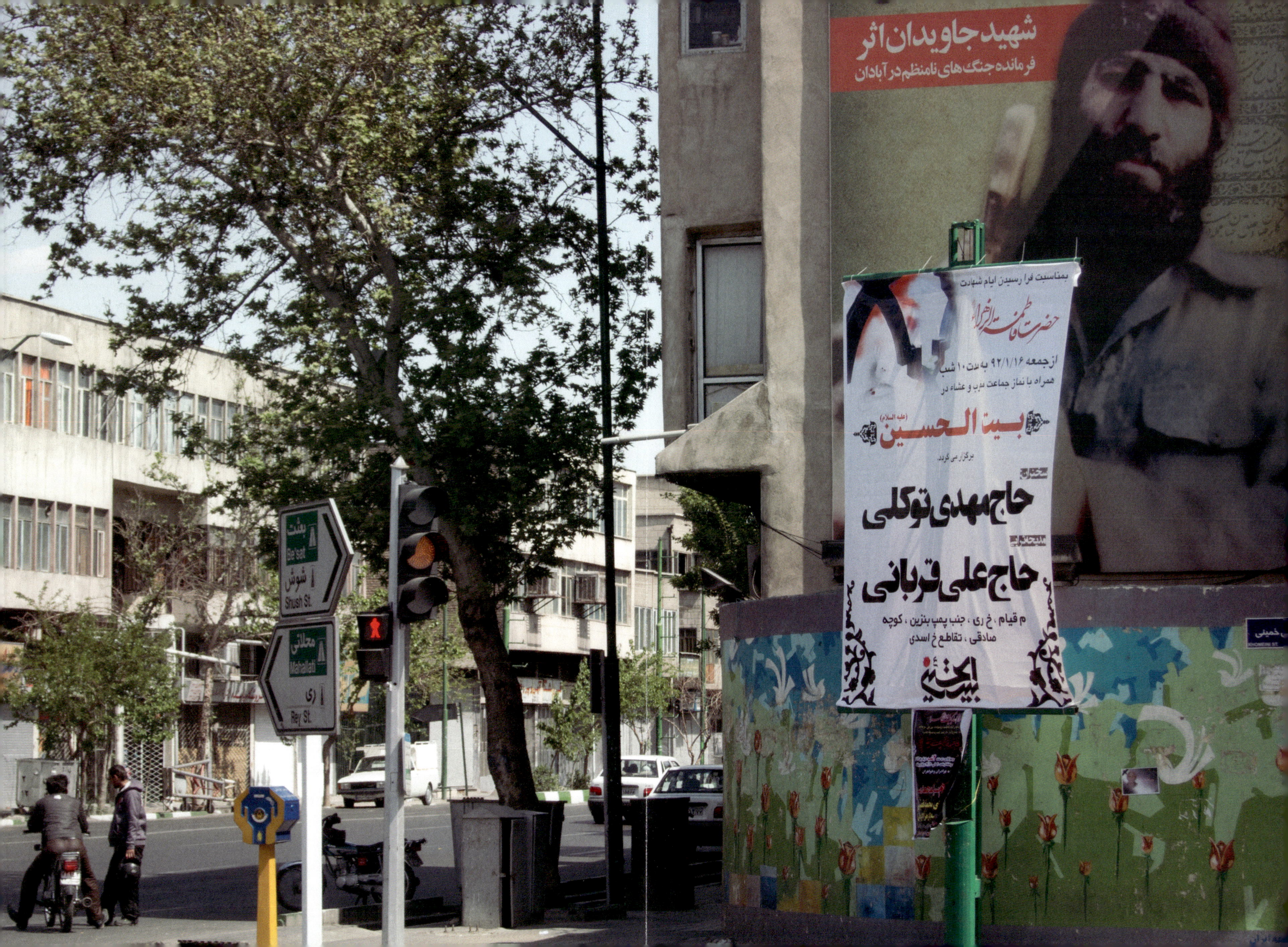

شهید جاویدان اثر
فرمانده جنگ های نامنظم در آبادان
بمناسبت فرا رسیدن ایام شهادت
حضرت فاطمة الزهرا
از جمعه ۹۲/۱/۱۶ به مدت ۱۰ شب
همراه با نماز جماعت مغرب و عشاء در
بیت الحسین (علیه السلام)
برگزار می گردد.
حاج مهدی توکلی
حاج علی قربانی
م قیام ، خ ری ، جنب پمپ بنزین ، کوچه
صادقی ، تقاطع خ اسدی
بعثت
Be'sat
شوش
Shush St.
محلاتی
Mahallati
ری
Rey St.

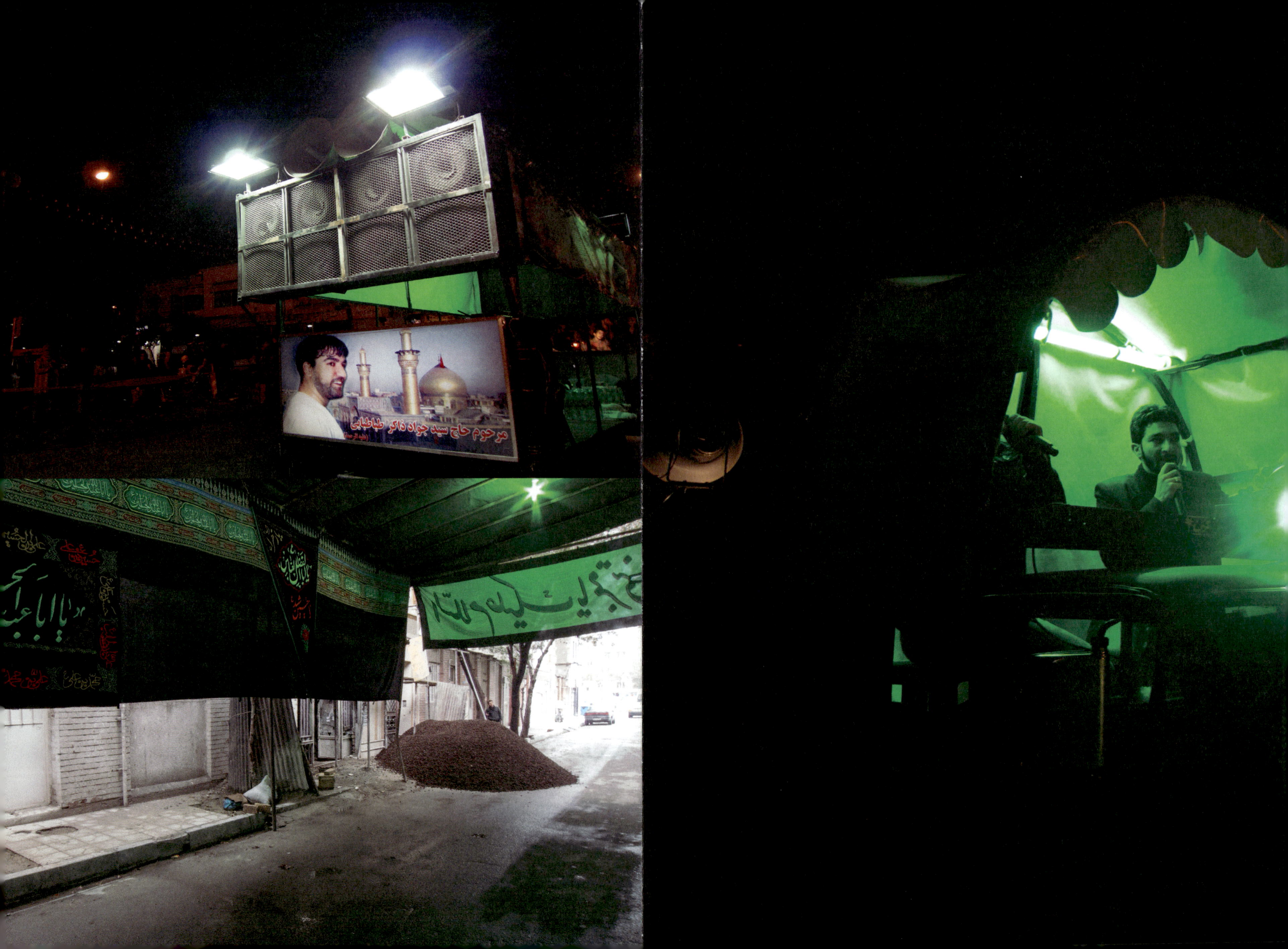
مرحوم حاج سید جواد ذاکر طباطبایی

"Just as I am, so are they;
Just as they are, so am I."
— Perry Schmidt-Leukel [13]

"To be verified by all things is to let the body and mind of the self and the body and mind of others drop off."
— Genjokoan, Dogen [14]

13. Perry Schmidt-Leukel, "Das Problem von Gewalt und Krieg in der buddhistischen Ethik", *Dialog der Religionen,* 1996, vol. 6, nr. 2, pp. 122-140

14. Shōbōgenzō, Eihei Dōgen, essay Genjōkōan (1233)

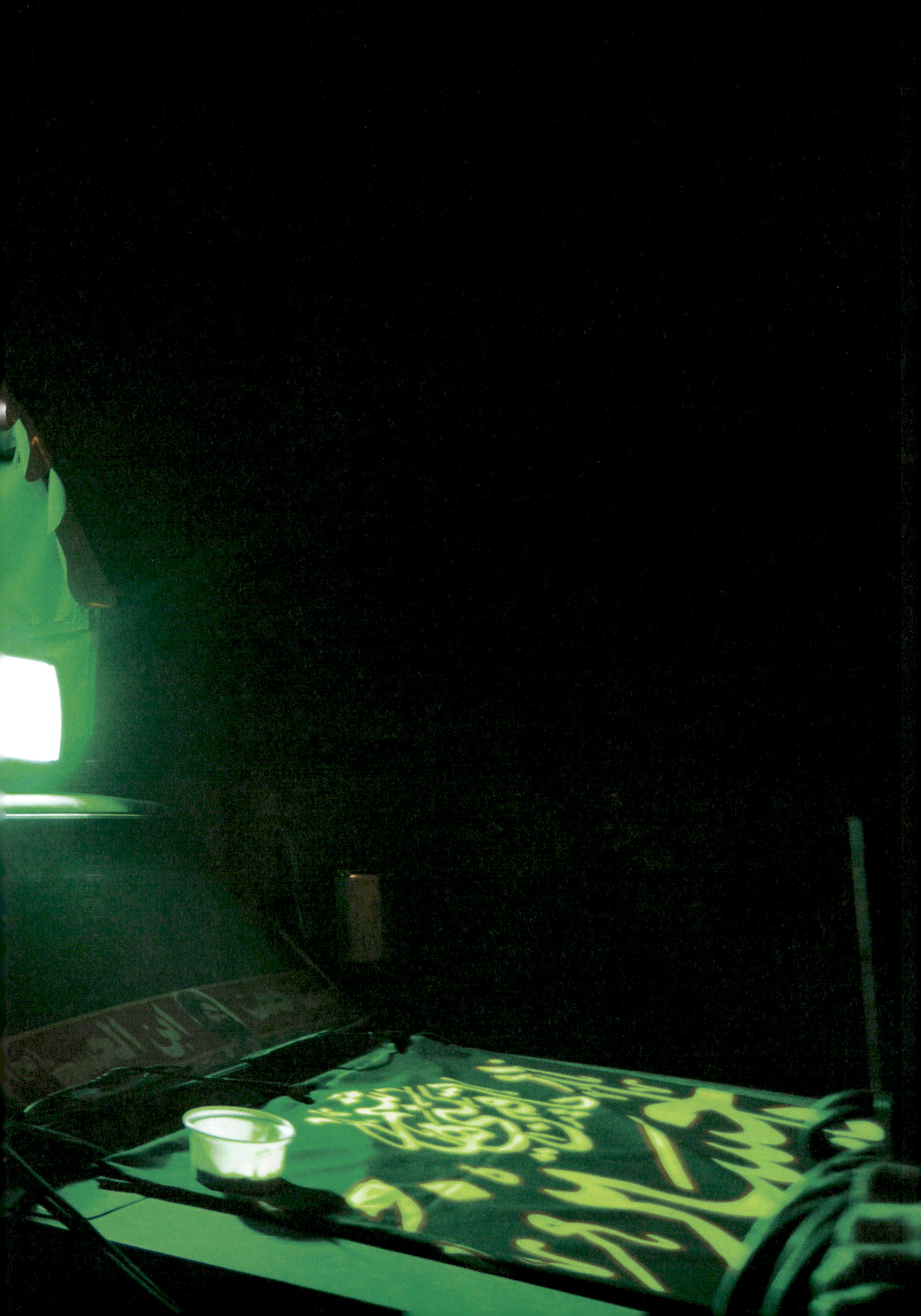

During a 1978 encounter at a Zen temple in Japan, Foucault remarked that this was "the end of the era of Western philosophy. Thus if philosophy of the future exists, it must be born outside of Europe or equally born in consequence of meetings and impacts between Europe and non-Europe".[15]

"It is not that religion is delusional by nature, not that the individual, beyond present-day religion, rediscovers his most suspect psychological origins. But religious delusion is a function of the secularization of culture: religion may be the object of delusional belief insofar as the culture of a group no longer permits the assimilation of religious or mystical beliefs in the present context of experience."
— Michel Foucault [16]

15. Janet Afary & Kevin B. Anderson, *Foucault and the Iranian Revolution: Gender and the Seductions of Islamism,* p. 2 (University of Chicago Press, 2005)

16. Michel Foucault, *Mental illness and psychology* (University of California Press, 1976)

Iran does not only have Persepolis as a testament to a heroic past but also poetry. During the revolution, the left-wing intellectual Shariati purged the spiritual facet of the Kerbala myth of all mystical elements.[17] Any poetry lecture that would stem from Sufi traditions and its followers would be avoided and the “right” use of death in the service of justice would be emphasised.

Poetry was turned into discourse and discourse became ideology.

The right use of death has a metaphorical meaning in Sufi tradition and essentially comes down to the death of the ego. It does not account for the destruction of the body as its vessel. The rise of solidarity during the revolution unwittingly strengthened the antagonism with those that found themselves outside of this group, including those who sought a symbolic rather than a literal reading of poetry. The social consequences emerged once the excitement of the uprising had died down. Many Sufi sects distanced themselves from the new policy.

Historically, protest was rife in the mystic houses established during Arab domination in the 10th century. Ta’ziyeh has its roots in mysticism, which it fuses with ancient mourning ceremonies that predate the Kerbala myth. Mysticism’s pursuit of “unification of contradictions” can also be traced in aspects of Ta’ziyeh, such as the simultaneous handling of different times and places. It is a performance of multidimensionality in which spectators transform into actors and vice versa.[18]

Mysticism in Iran is a fragmented concept. Mysticism has an uncomfortable relationship with language: it needs language but language actually destroys it. The essence of mysticism is the experience of being “where no tongue can speak of it”. Concepts confine; they create divisive thinking.

The poetry of Iranian mysticism has not been spared from being pressed into the service of furthering political ends. For its part, mysticism is a powerful force in hindering orthodox thinking within a political discourse that aims to mould a fixed identity. Some of the Sufi orders, including the Gonabadi and Nimatullahi, have suffered greatly under the current orthodox regime, while others have been given more freedoms. The strategies are unclear and asking questions rarely leads to adequate answers. Different orders are pitted against each other, go underground or stay safe by using a camouflaged discourse. Everyone keeps their cards close to their chests. Instead of proclaiming who they are, the facades of Sufi meeting houses are discretely anonymous, usually with locked front doors. If you’re very lucky, there will be an entrance at the back. The idea that there is a split between Islam and mysticism, as if the two things can be separated, is probably too simplistic. Mysticism is the basis of all religion.[19]

The application of the rules and the excessive attention to these rules may be orthodox. Mysticism, or the internalisation of the divine, is more acceptable and comprehensible for westerners since it conforms to their views on the private nature of spirituality. Mysticism is considered a separate aspect of traditional religions. But it is not a personal matter in Iran. Nor is it an individual business: it is a powerful drive that uses social tentacles to challenge the authoritarian and hierarchical and assert a common ground of unity.

Some of the orders have a problematic relationship with the authorities. It is impossible to figure out what exactly is going on, aside from the obvious observation that this is a liberal versus an orthodox view. It is like struggling in quicksand: with every new fragment of information, the overall picture becomes more muddied and out of reach. Every statement, conversation or occurrence can be read in two ways. This

particular social paranoia arises from the sense of being hunted. The insecurity is the result of not fitting in with the ideology of the ruling authority. When people are in such vulnerable positions, there is a strong argument for forming groups.
It is not only the Sufi communities that speak in paranoid terms: so do the authorities, though from a different perspective. The tighter the strictures of an ideology, the faster the self-generated outsiders will be seen as dissidents. There is a constant interaction between real threat and misplaced distrust. Where there is armour, it will be attacked.

Sufi schools and Iranian history are deeply entwined and this is their best protection from an intolerant regime.
The radical placelessness and timelessness that are inherent to Sufism and mysticism are a mental state. Language can make it communicable but also vulnerable. Through language alone, it remains essentially misunderstood.

17. Ali Shariati Mazinani, sociologist, historian, revolutionary, °Kahak (Iran) (1952-1977)

18 Khosrow Shahriari, *Breaking Down Borders and Bridging Barriers: Iranian Taziyeh Theatre*, (University of New South Wales, 2006)

19. Interview with Jonas Slaats, writer, social activist, °1980 (Ghent); author of *Soefi's, punkers & poëten. Een christen op reis door de islam* (Altiora, 2015)

Note (6)

A view with room

The pre-verbal field of mysticism is often described as a field behind a veil or curtain. It is the basic principle that both establishes and questions the narrative and thus frees it from being set in stone.
The veil - the image and the language - can be communicated. That means that it can also be mediatised and instrumentalised. But that which is behind it is free. It is the space where the one is completely the other.
The borders between living room and street are untenable. This is not for ideological reasons but through being encapsulated in a broader field where each is equal and even non-existent as separate spaces. This field has no inside or outside. It is atopic.
In mysticism, the coordinates of time and space are imaginary. While bodies are indeed present and are the bearers of stories that continually shape the course of events, they are also perceived as an undivided unity. Everything is instantaneous. The moment is not understood as an unfathomable point between the past and the future. All that makes someone an individual dis-

solves and as a result, the past and the future are prod-
ucts of the all-encompassing now.

n her book *Mysticism and Resistance,* Dorothee Sölle[2] argues that in the current economic hierarchy, our at-achment to the ego has become the foundation of ou lives. The individual is not seen as a free agent but in-stead as infinitely exploitable. In her book, the word "resistance" is not concerned with the fire of revolu-tion but with endeavouring to shape a different way o life. Resistance refers to any ordinary aspect of life tha does not seek to conform.

Secular mysticism does not conform with staged indi-viduality. It combines contemplation with action. This form of mysticism recognises the ego as the ultimate prison warden (p. 291).

The perception of mysticism as an excuse to avoid re-ality owes much to the notion that religion is a private matter.

Asceticism is really an interruption, a withdrawal, a different relationship to things and so does not mean breaking the body over the wheel (p. 304).

t is the motion that goes from faster, bigger and more productive to slower, smaller and more aware (p. 306).

"The supremacy of the truth of now compared to all o planned history is the result of the fact that one uses the compass of being rather than having." (p. 351)

"Understanding mysticism as the jailbreak of the ego from self-exploitation is radically opposed to the basic tenets of capitalism and is the key to freedom in the true sense of the word." (p. 299)

The wide use of images and languages can be recoded "A view with room" has nothing to do with wanting a new car and "Be anything" is a mindset that doesn' need anything to accomplish itself.

When the city is reread as potentially mystical then its citizens cannot be reduced to a state of permanent pov-erty and neediness.

My original reason for visiting Iran was to investigate the political situation of the Sufis there and to analyse the public space. This led to a temporary construct, o thought experiment, for which I would refuse to see the other as a separate and "other" being.

n one way or another, images will present a dichotomy employ the method of juxtaposing photographs (here there and earlier/now) in order to expose meanings tha would not otherwise be there. This meaning is creat-ed by the interface and not by the pictures themselves terms of difference, of the dichotomy between subjective and objective: a dichotomy that a mystical perspective wipes out.

Photography is a tool I use to orientate myself. Photography is an exercise in contributing to the shaping of life. Photography, sound and words are resources that – when composed in certain ways – can function briefly as a thread through a labyrinth. For me personally, learning to live can seem like a form of spiritual politics that has the capacity – should some sort of dogmatism arise – to rearrange the thread at any moment. Mastering the Curtains has become an analysis of a coreless being. Mysticism cannot be a method as it questions all methods. I am intrigued by the radical nature of the mystical perspective. It is not an opposition to a specific ideology but to ideologies full stop. It is an exercise in blasting holes in imaginary prisons.

20. Dorothee Sölle, The Silent Cry: *Mysticism and Resistance,* (Fortress Press, 2001)

Recently, I got my hands on the philosopher Peter Sloterdijk's book You Must Change Your Life. My eyes immediately fell on this powerful paragraph:[21]

"I will show that a return *to* religion is as impossible as a return *of* religion - for the simple reason that no 'religion' or 'religions' exist, only misunderstood spiritual regimens, whether these are practiced in collectives - usually church, *ordo, umma, sangha* – or in customized forms – through interaction with the 'personal God' with whom the citizens of modernity are privately insured. Thus the tiresome distinction between 'true religion' and superstition loses its meaning. There are only regimens that are more and less capable and worthy of propagation. The false dichotomy of believers and unbelievers becomes obsolete and is replaced by the distinction between the practicing and the untrained, or those who train differently."

21. Peter Sloterdijk, *You Must Change Your Life,* translated by Wieland Hoban (Polity Press, 2012)

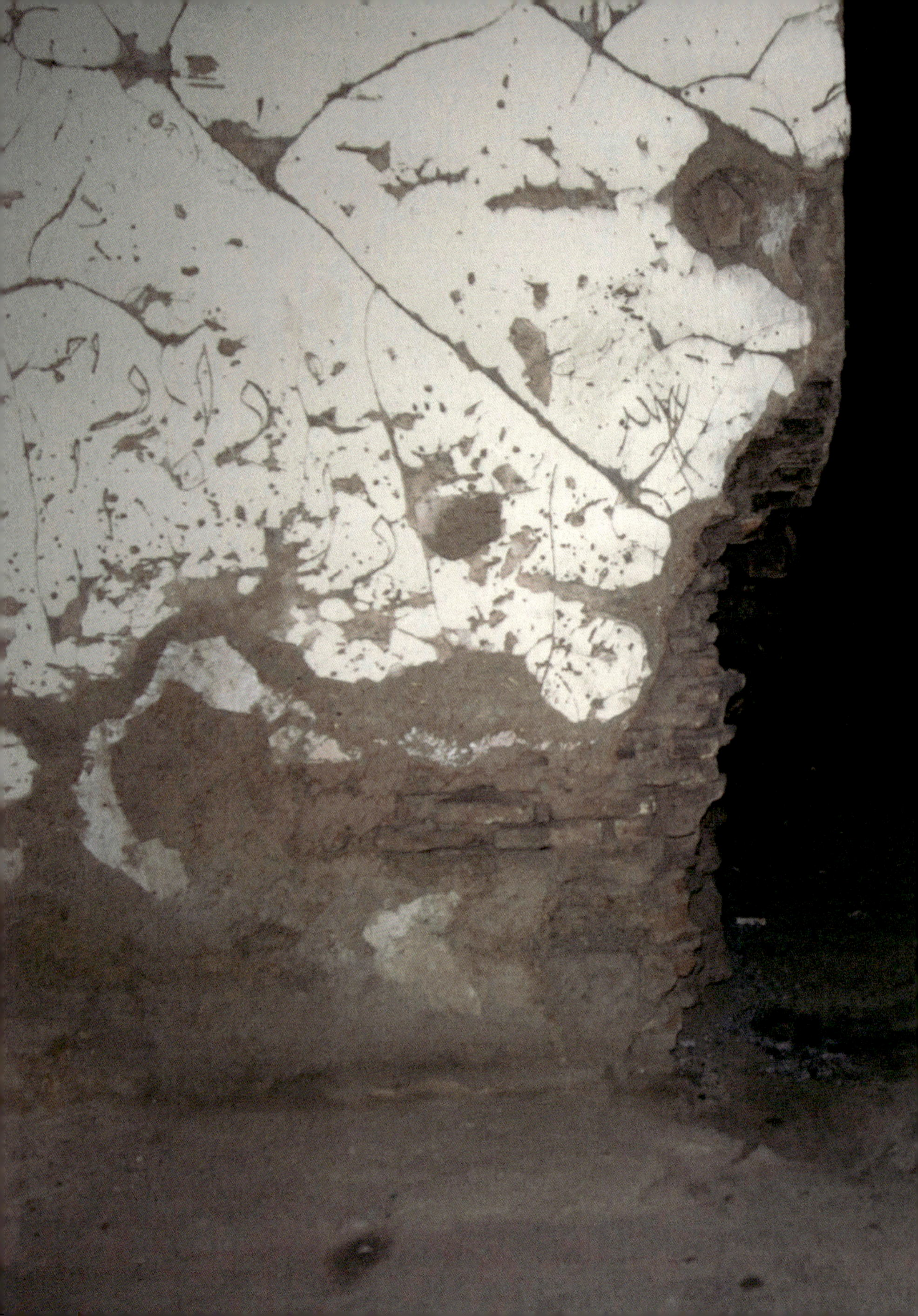

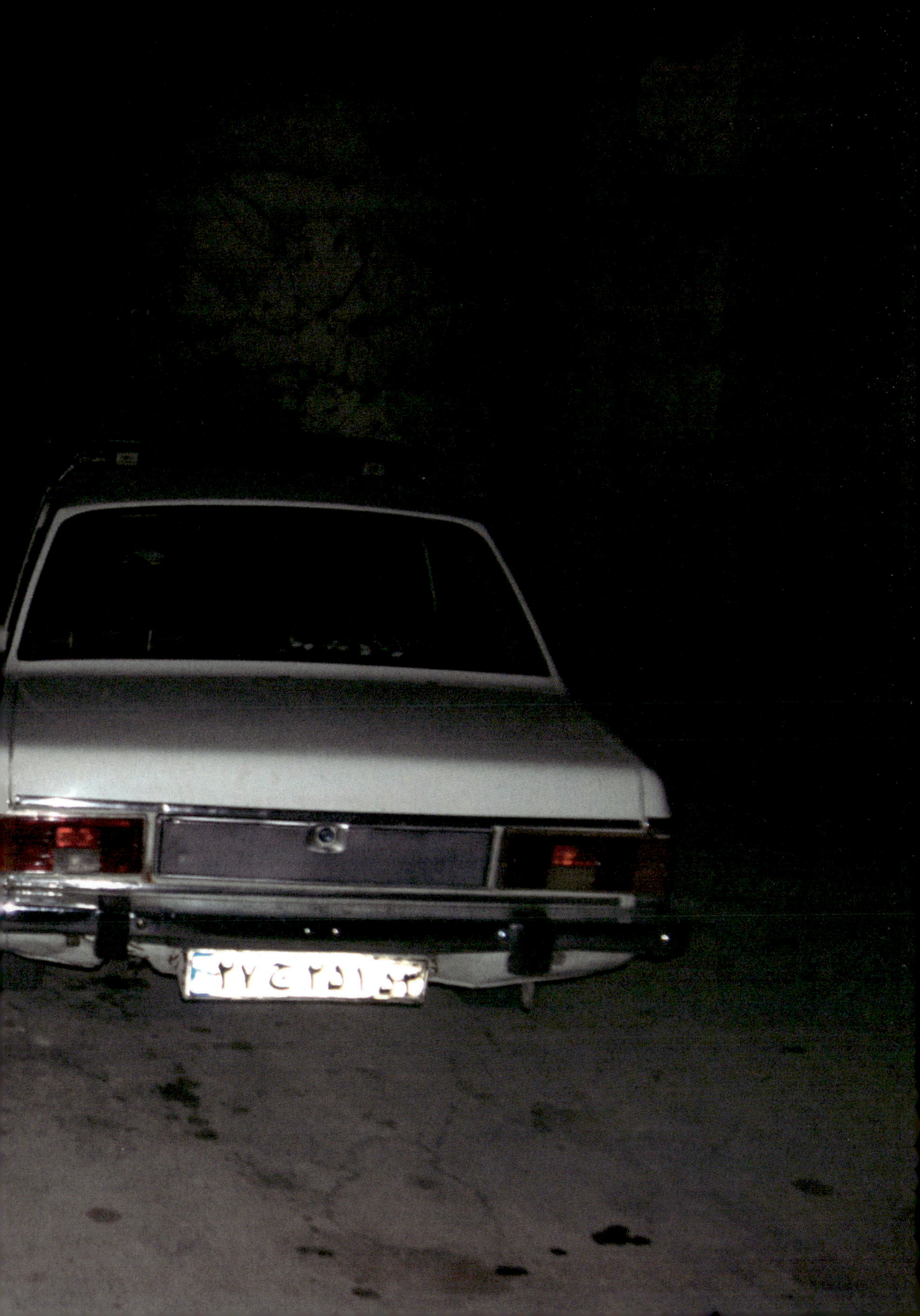
۲۷ ج ۲۵۱

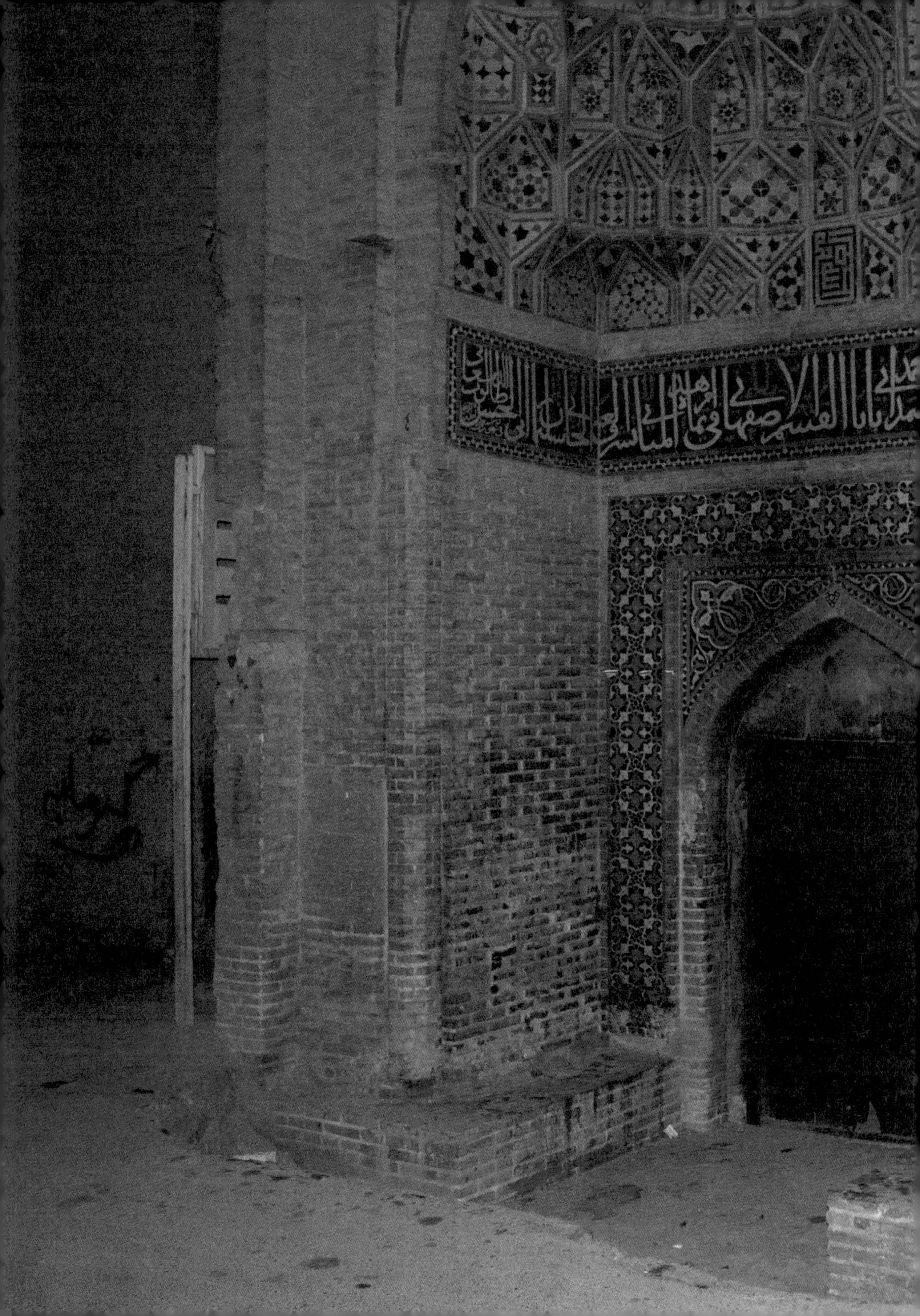

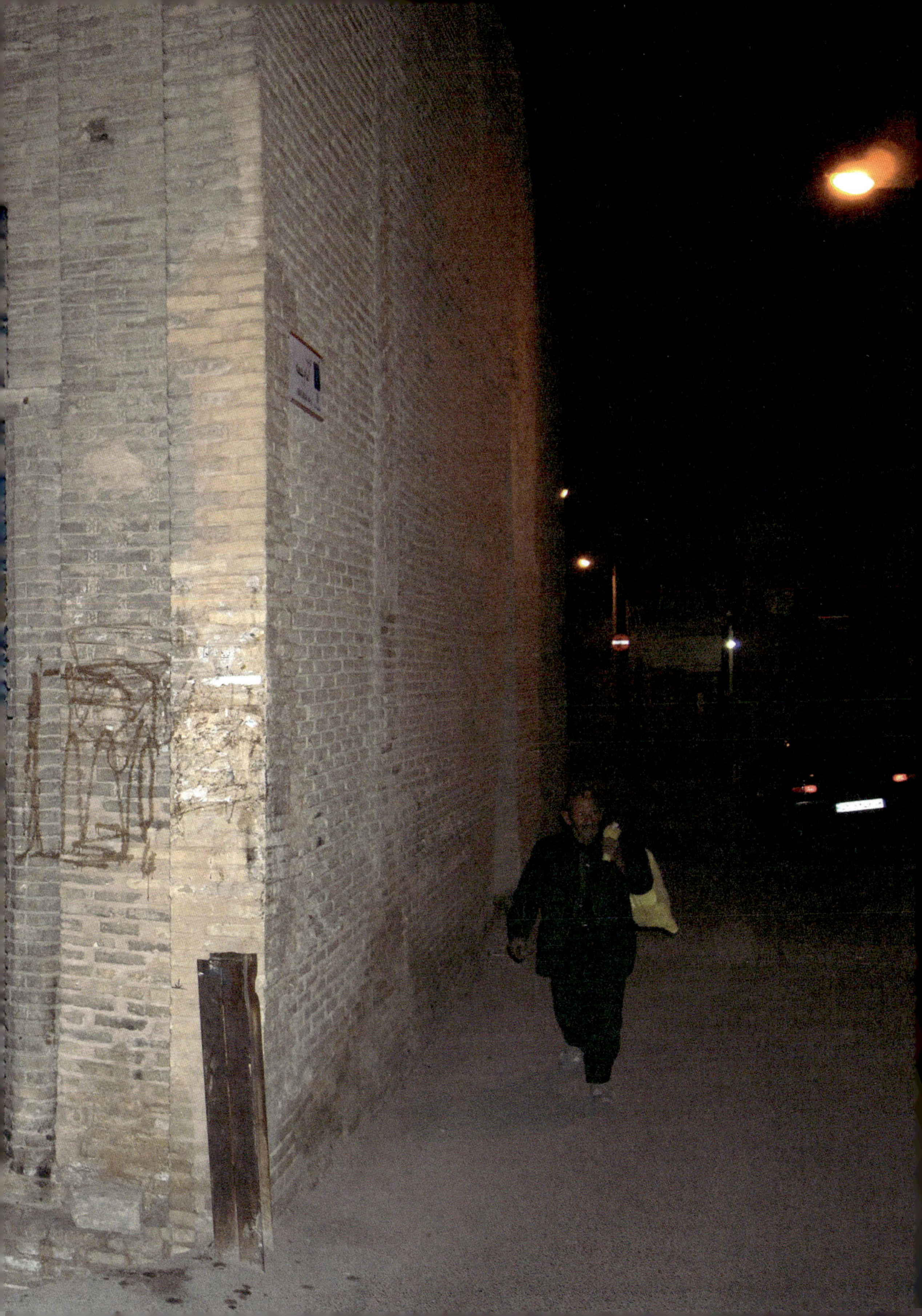

405 GLX

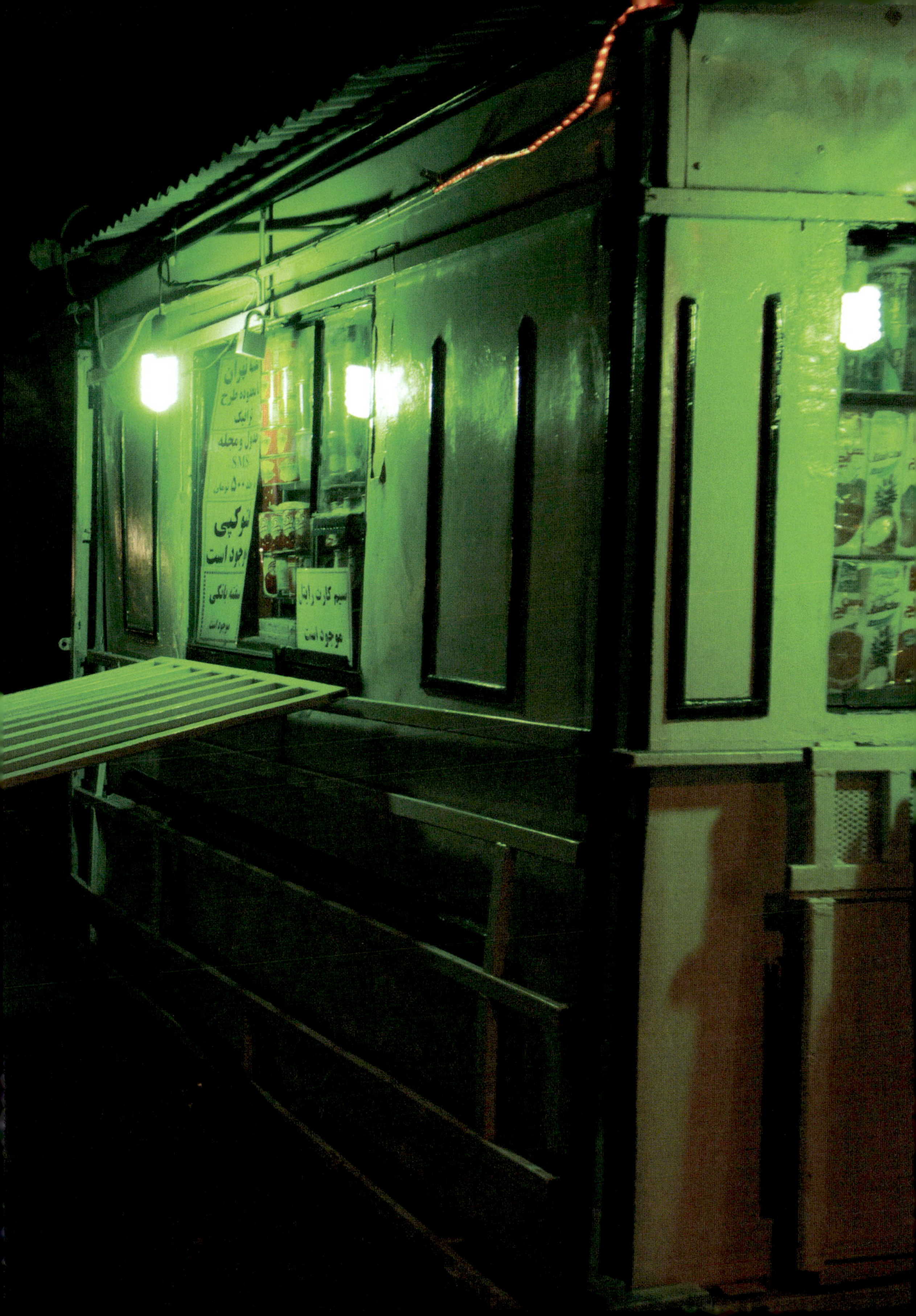
SMS
موجود است
سفته بانکی
موجود است
سیم کارت رایتل
موجود است

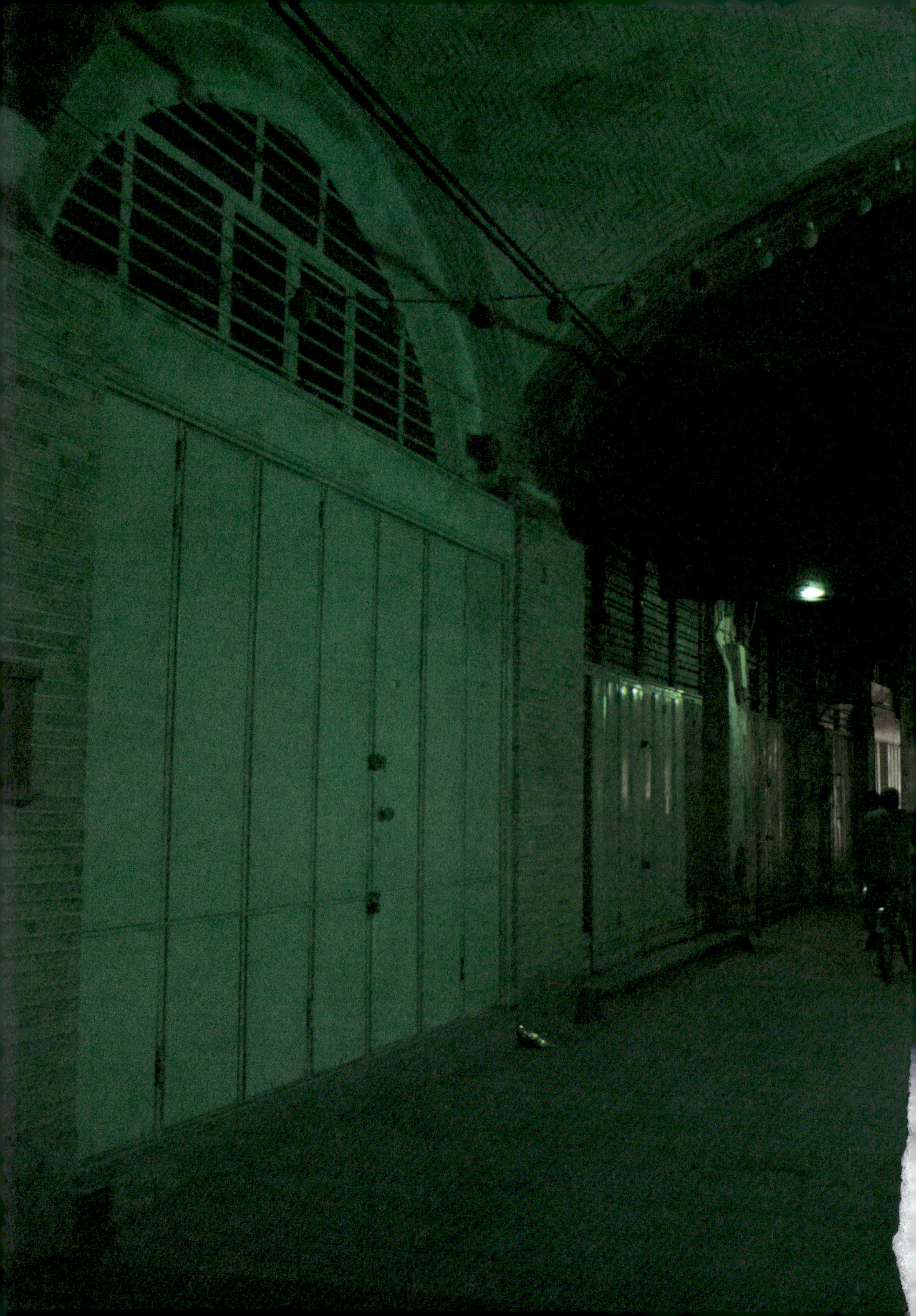

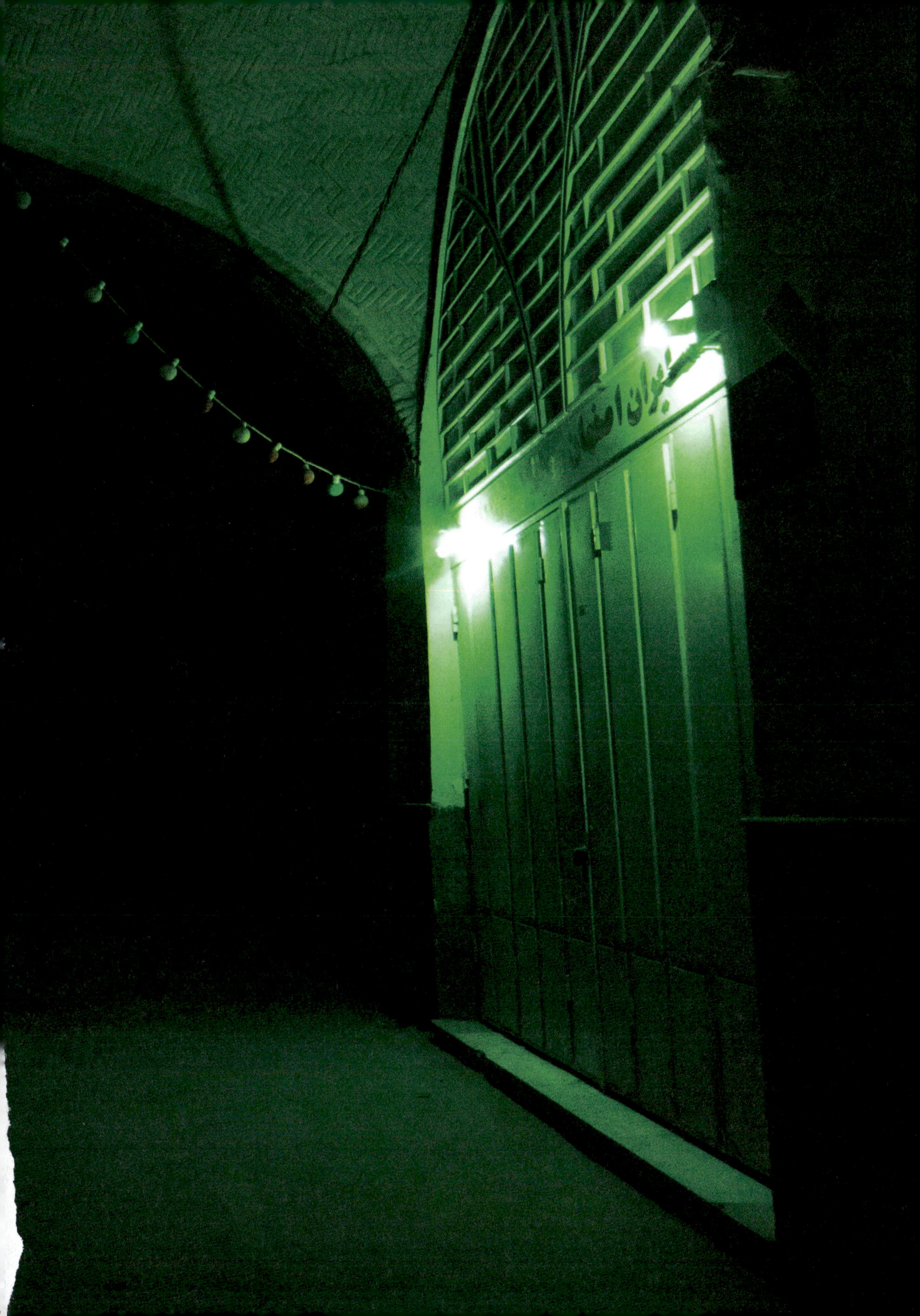

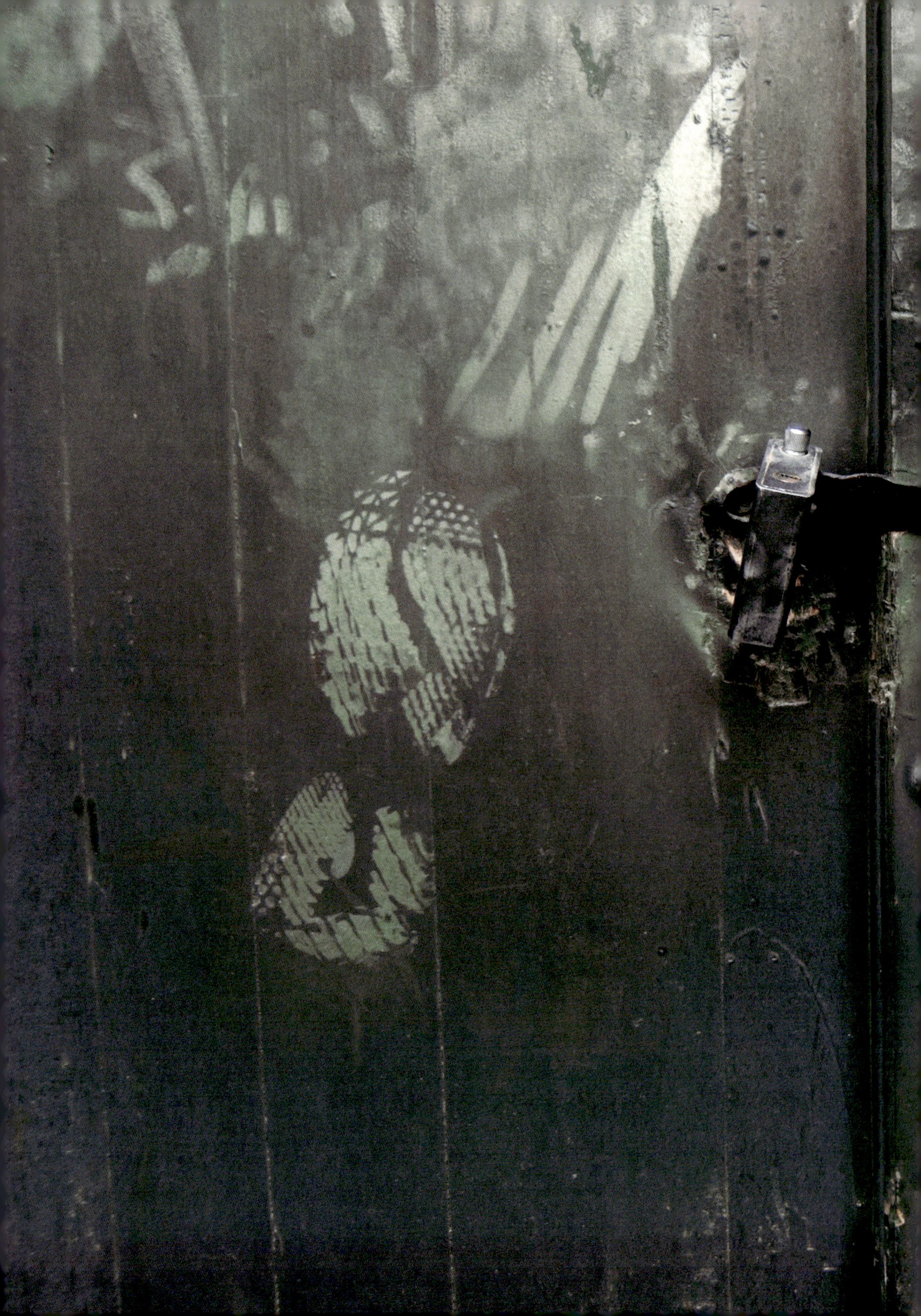

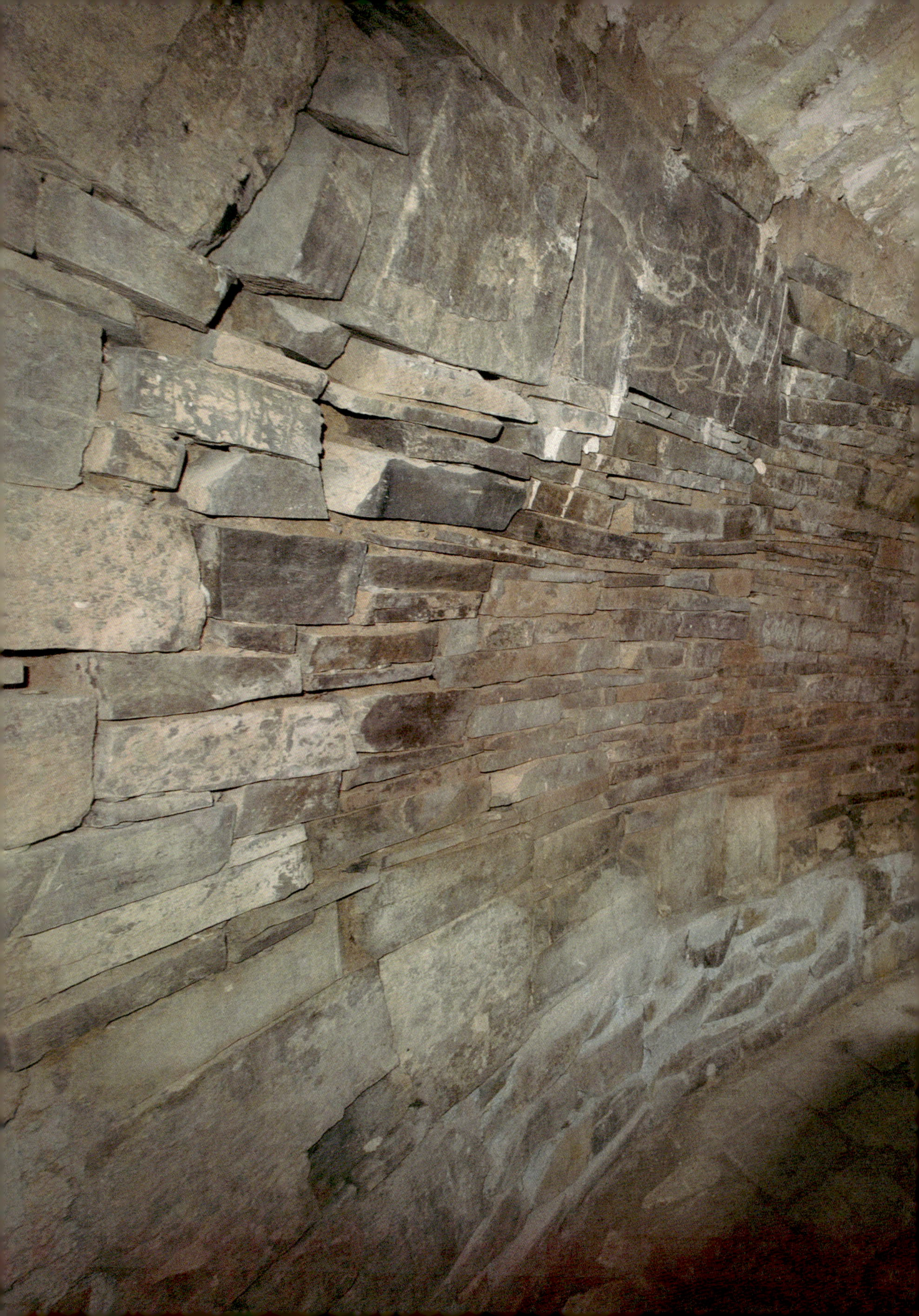

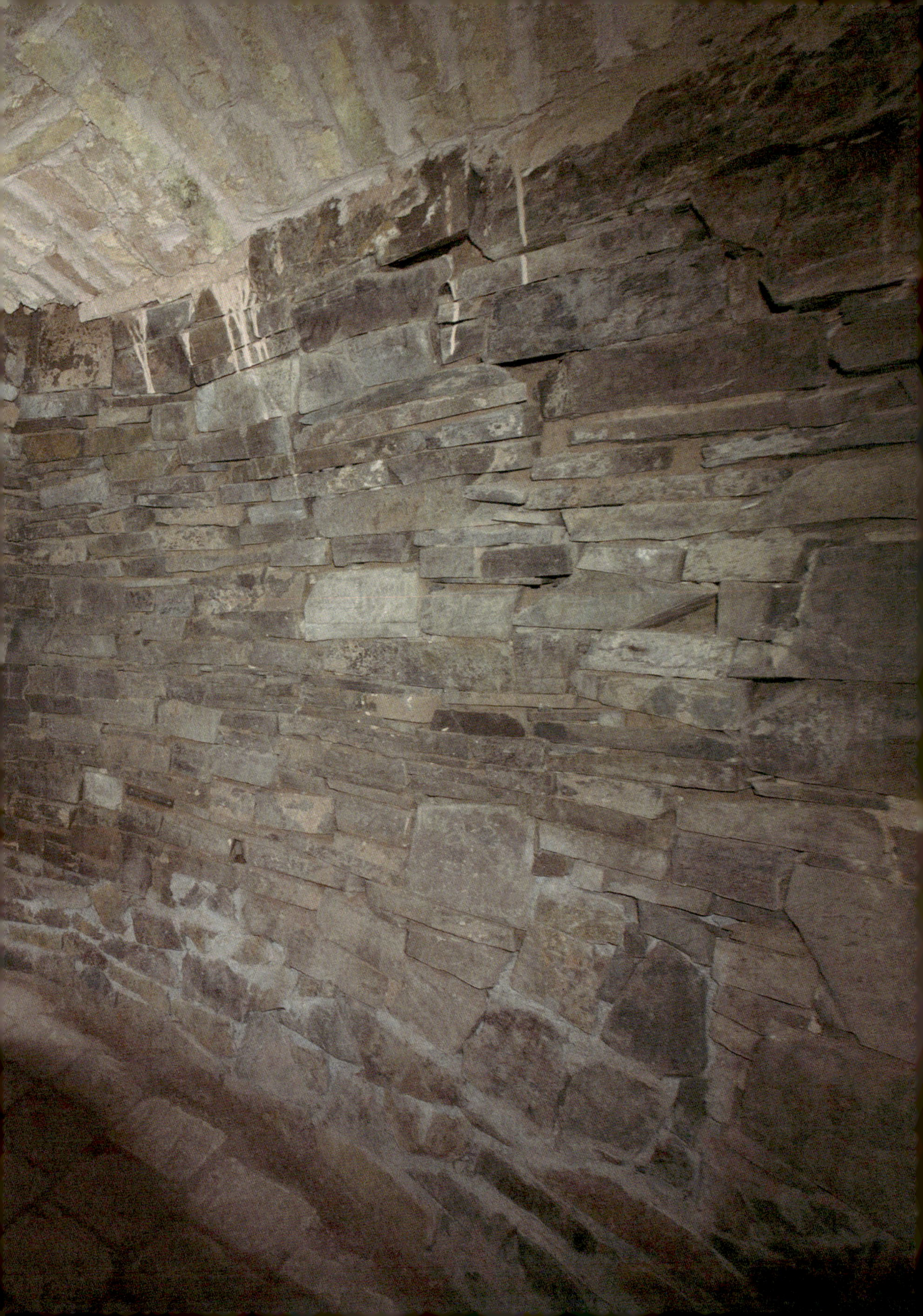

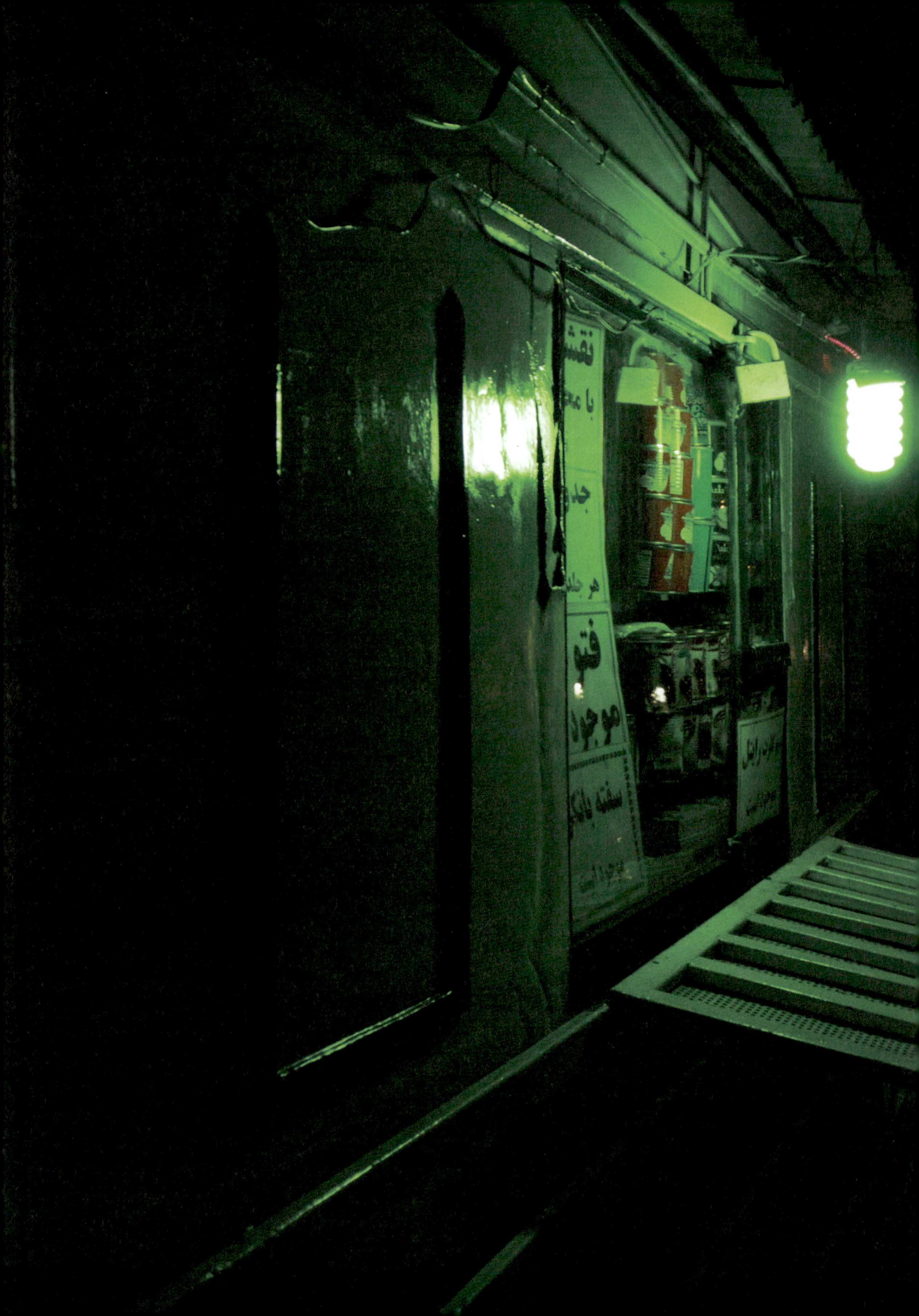
موجود
سفته

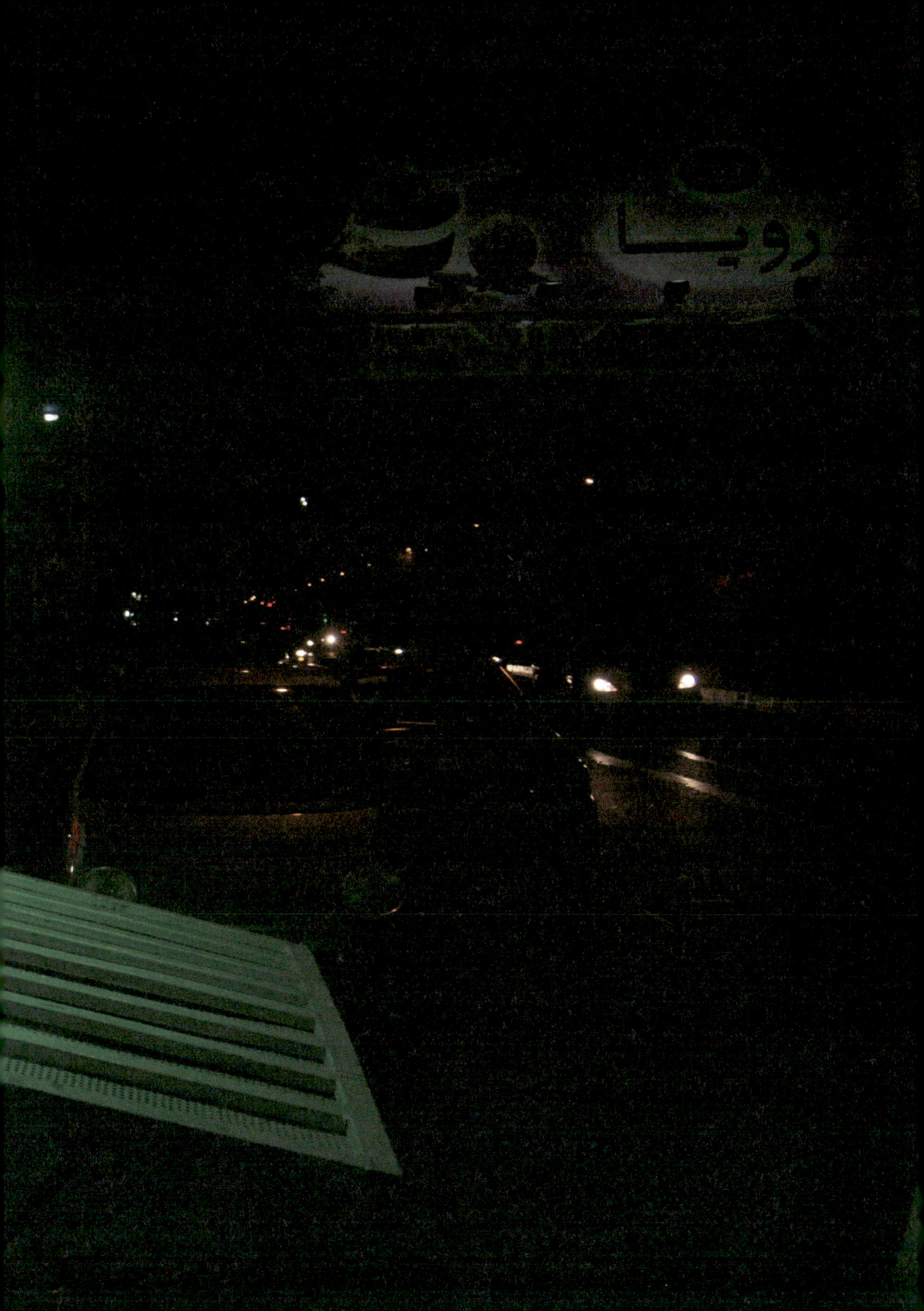

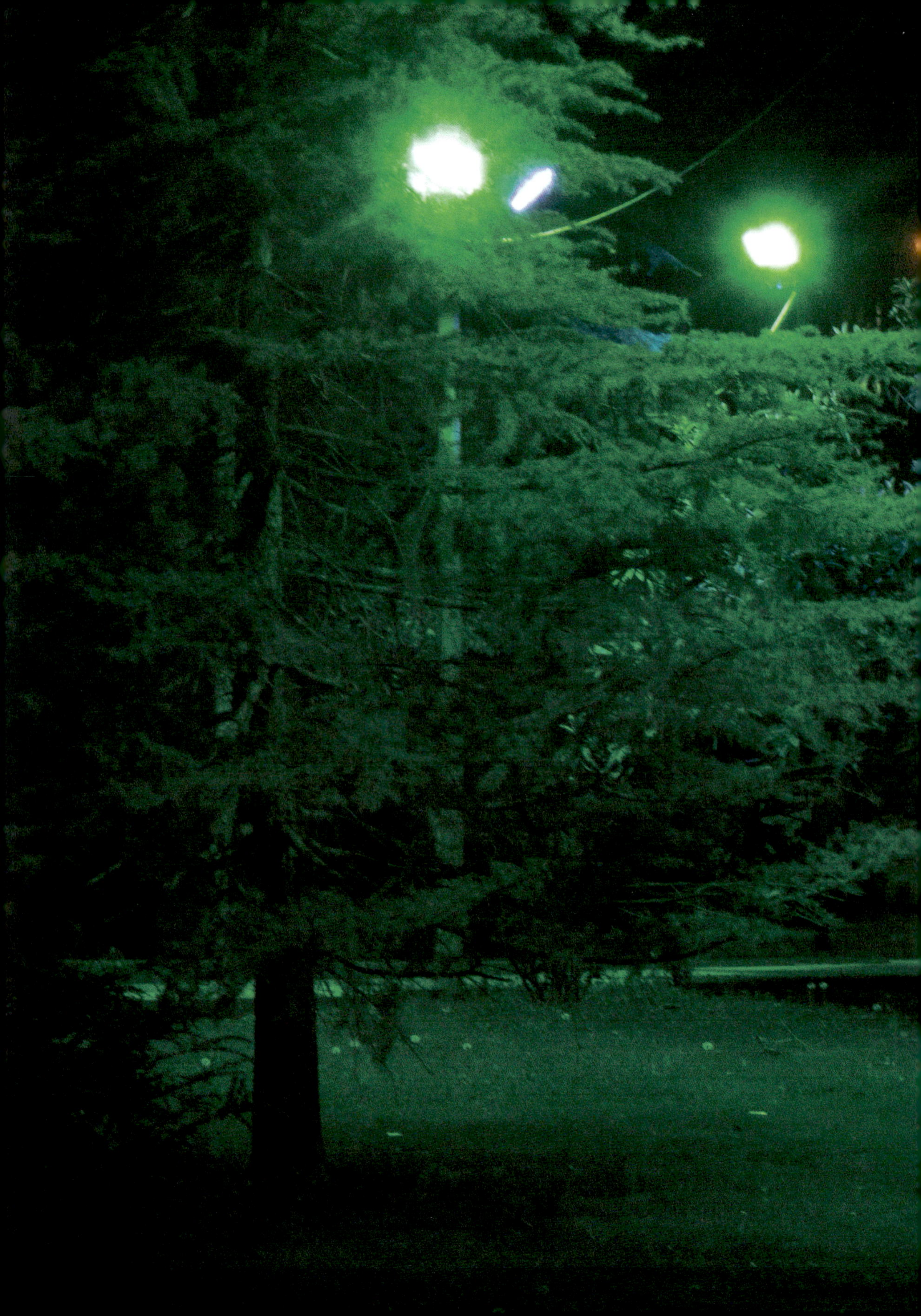

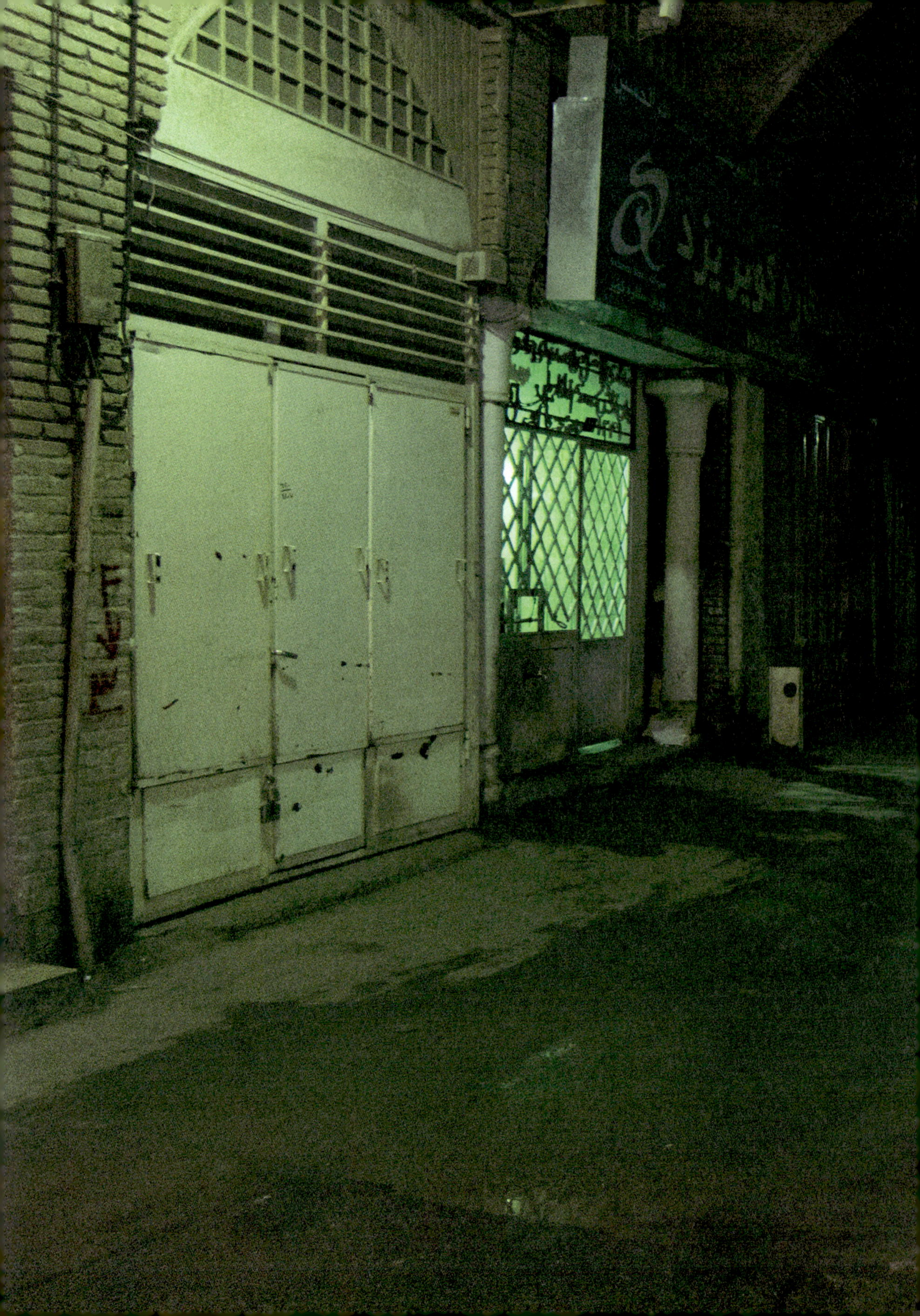

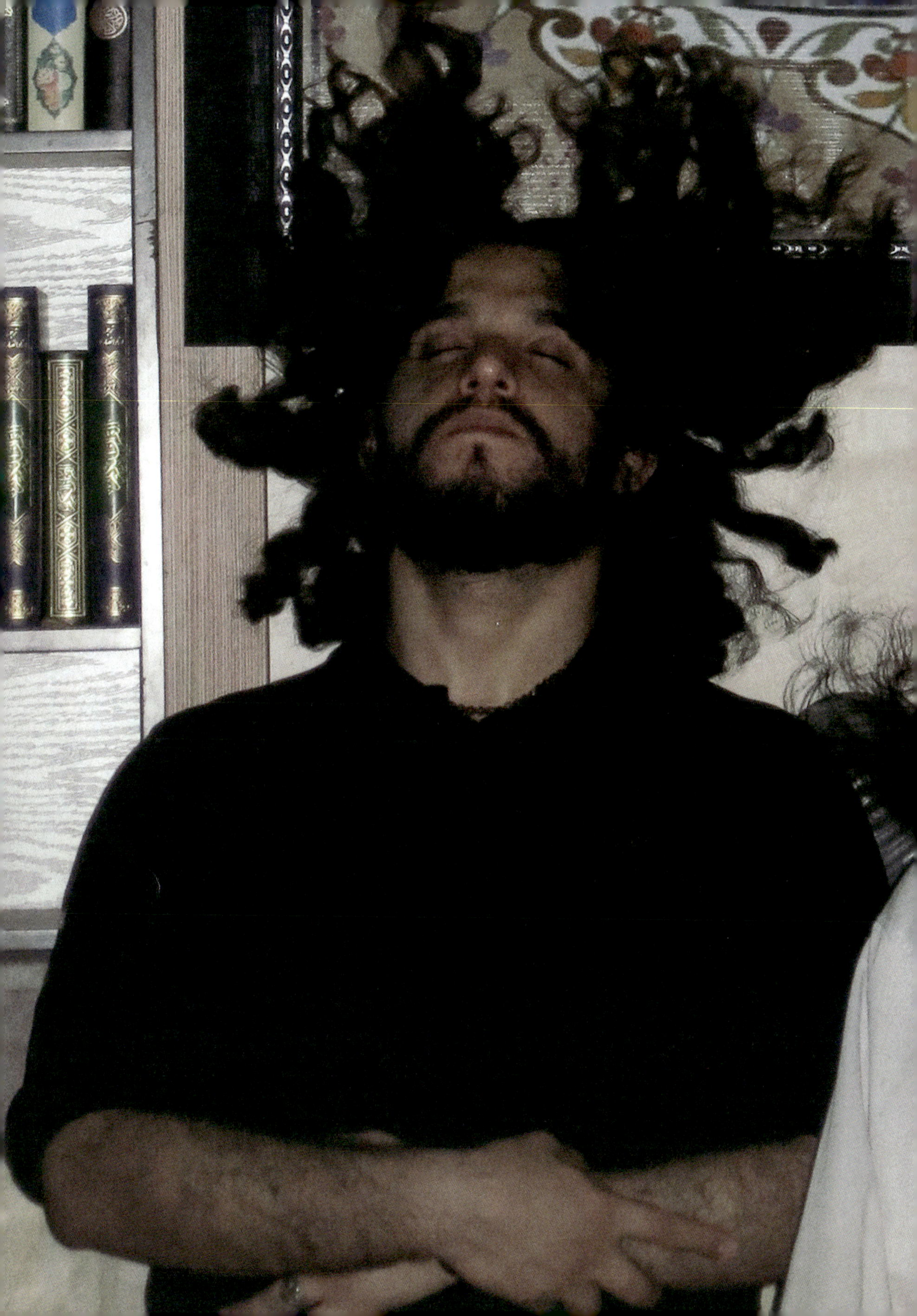

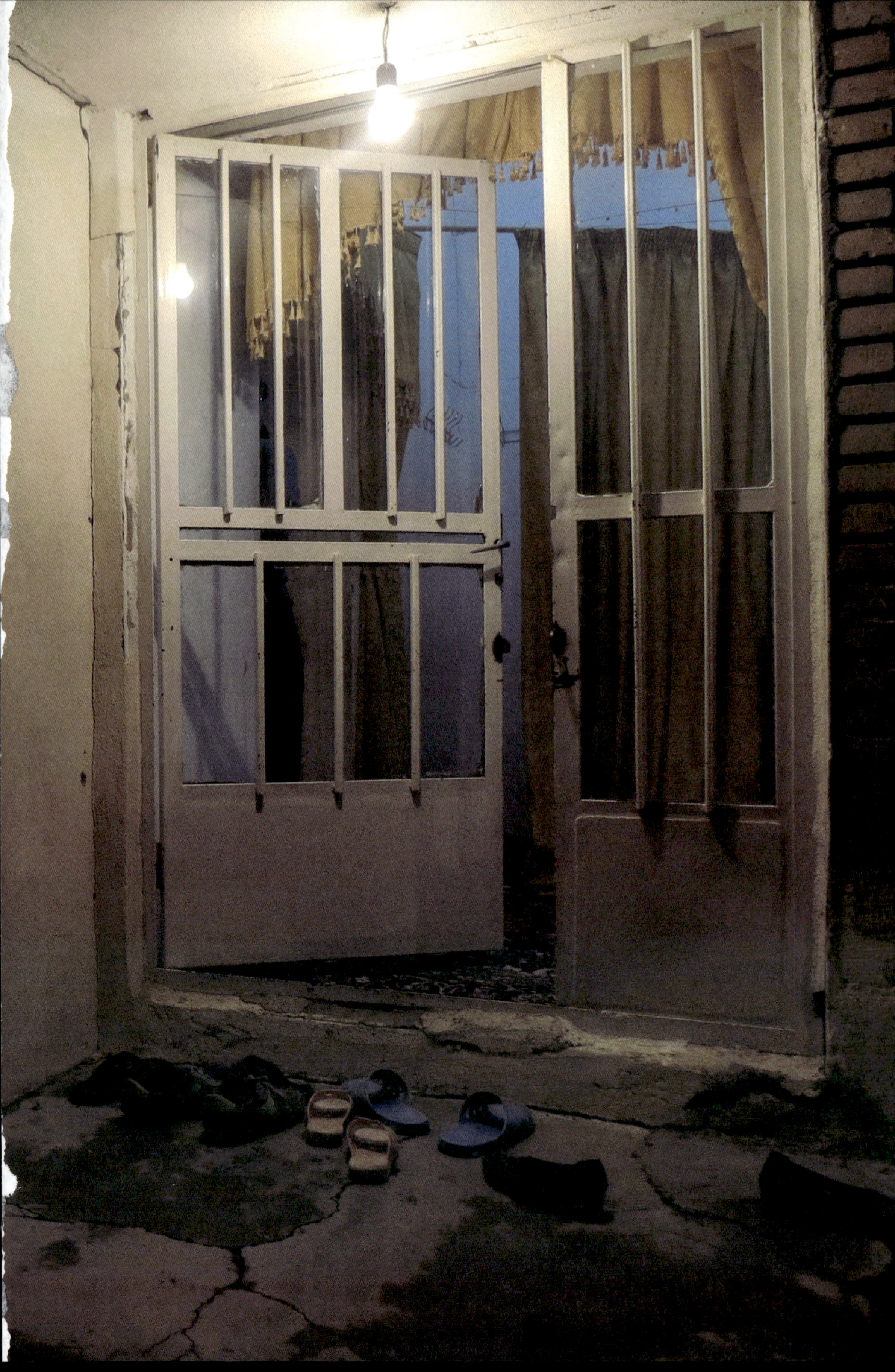

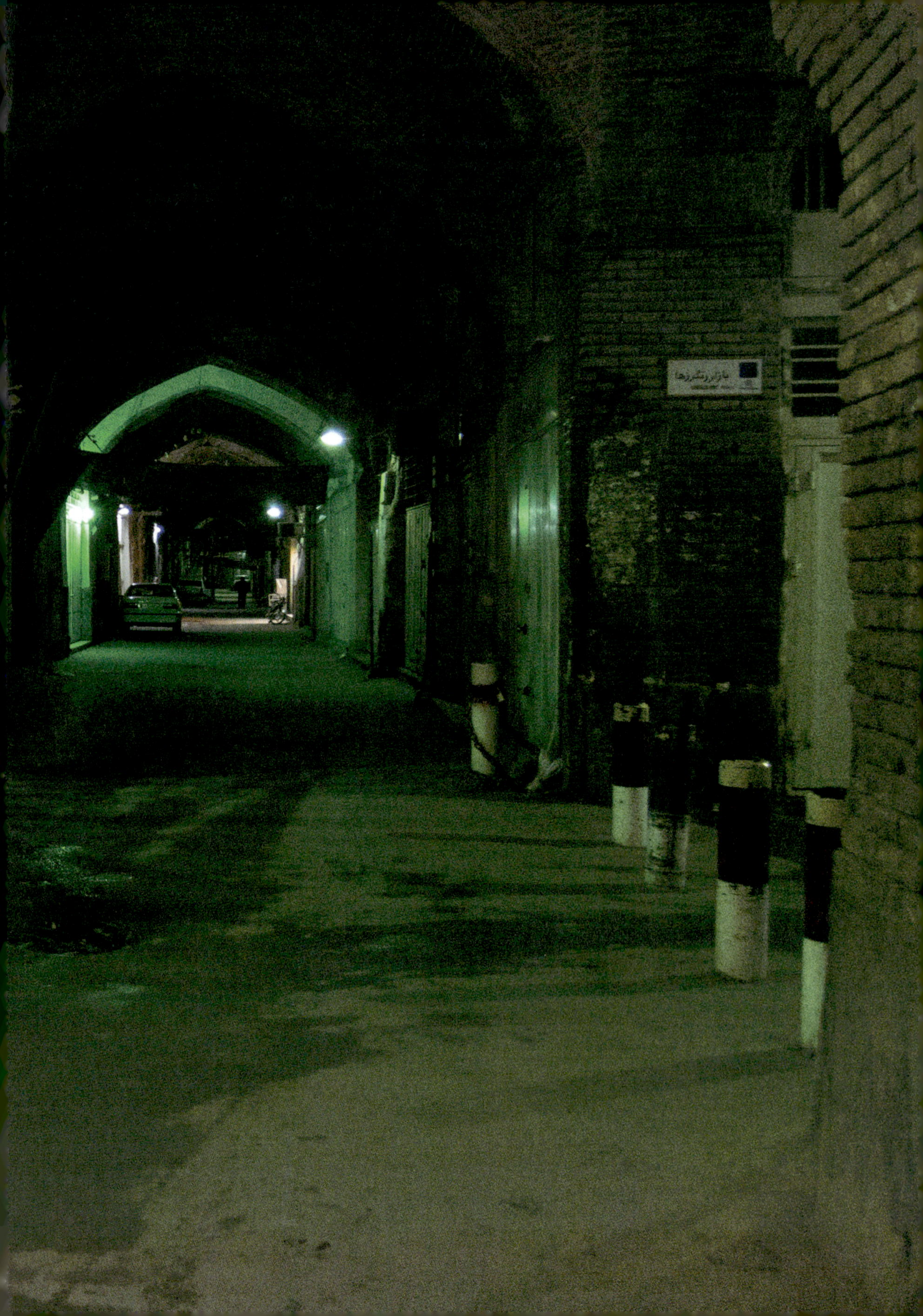

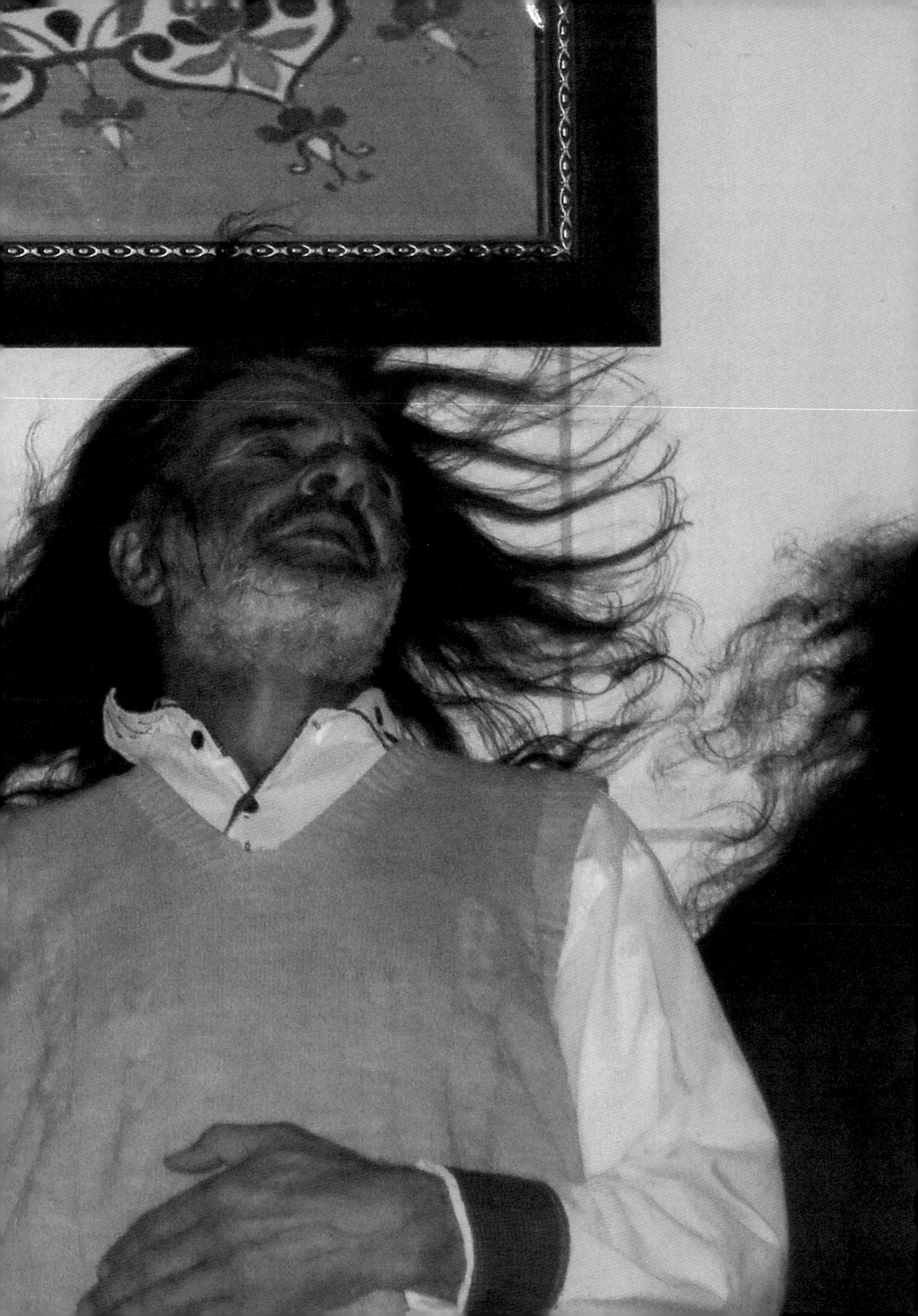

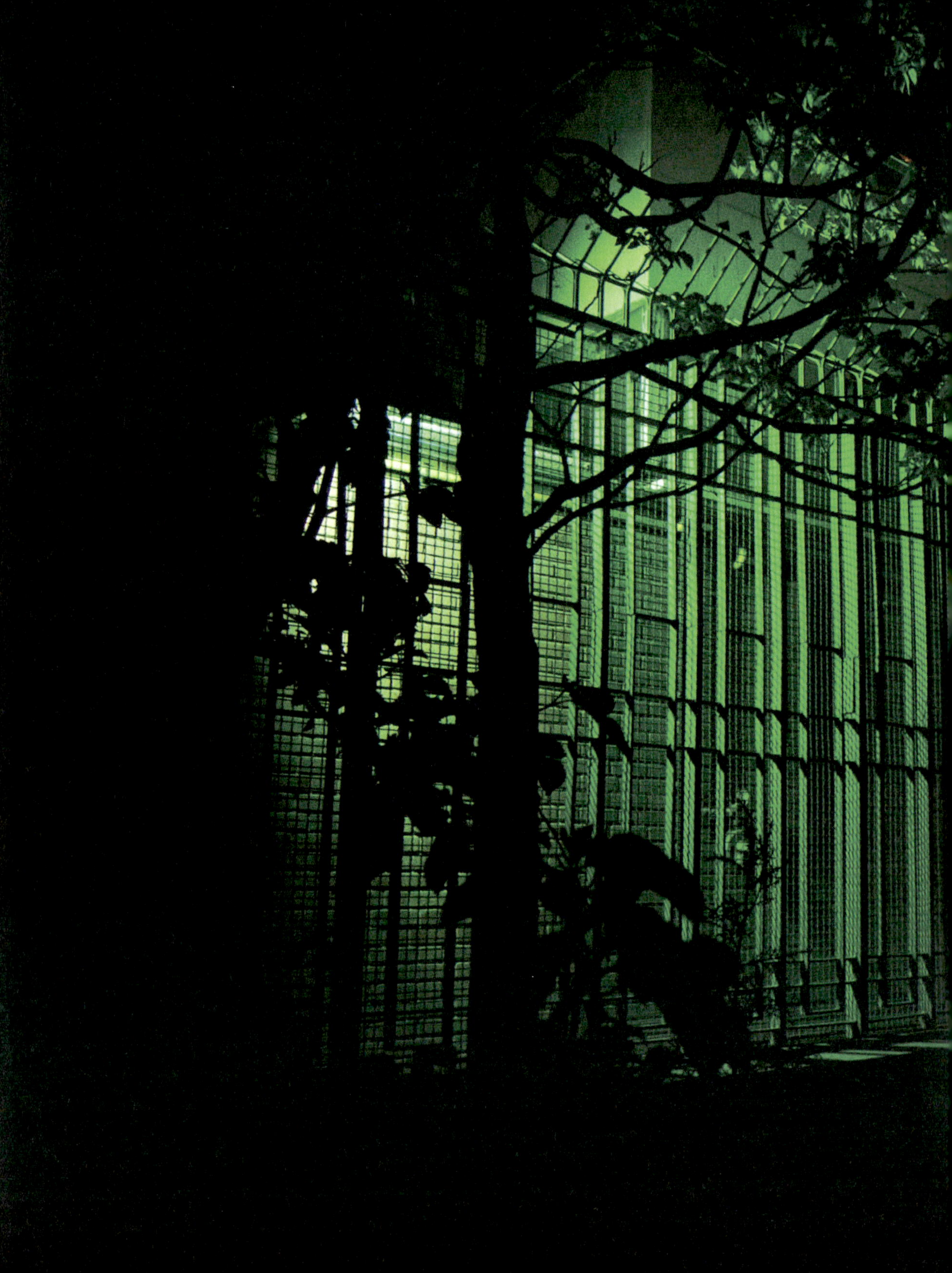

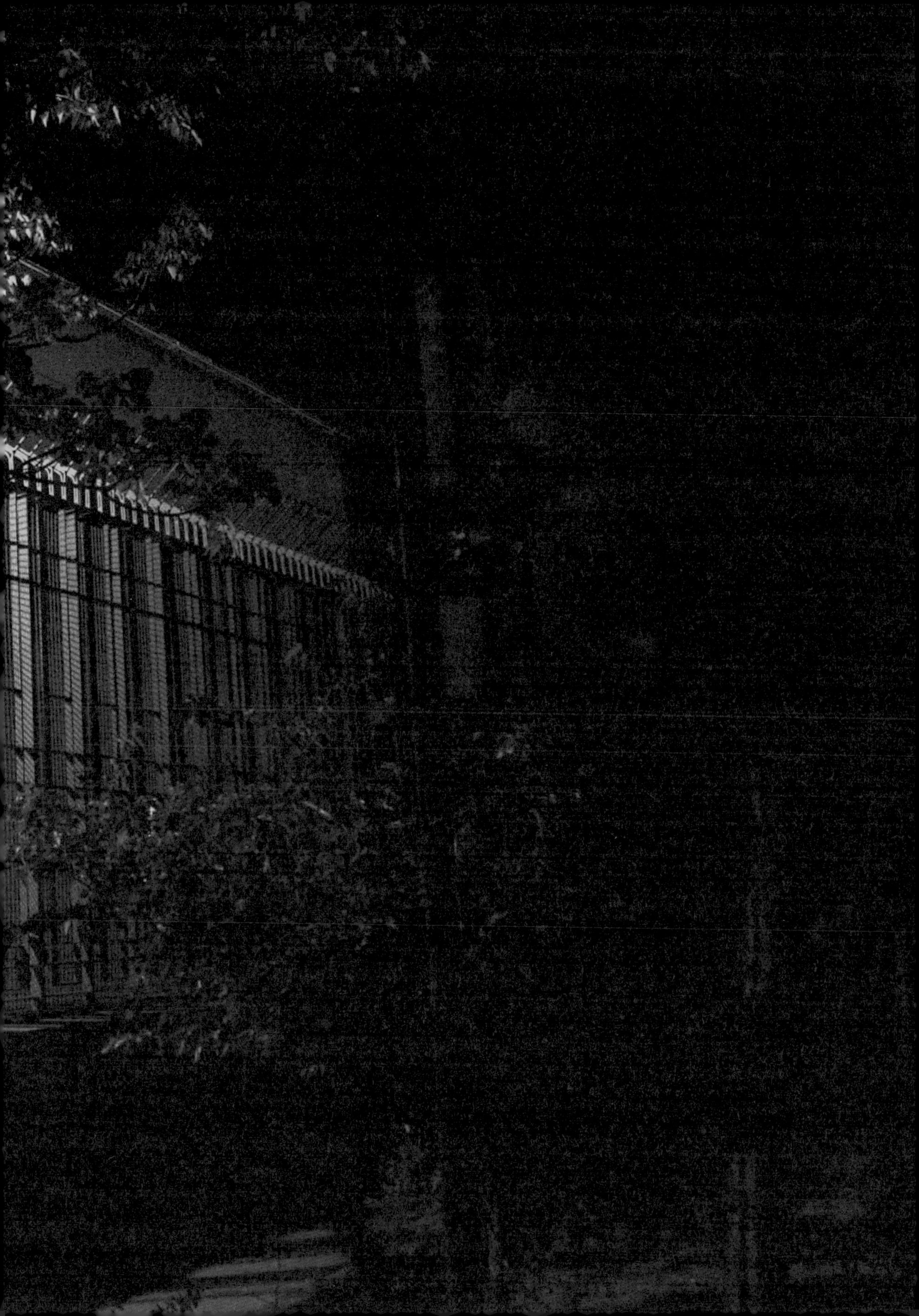

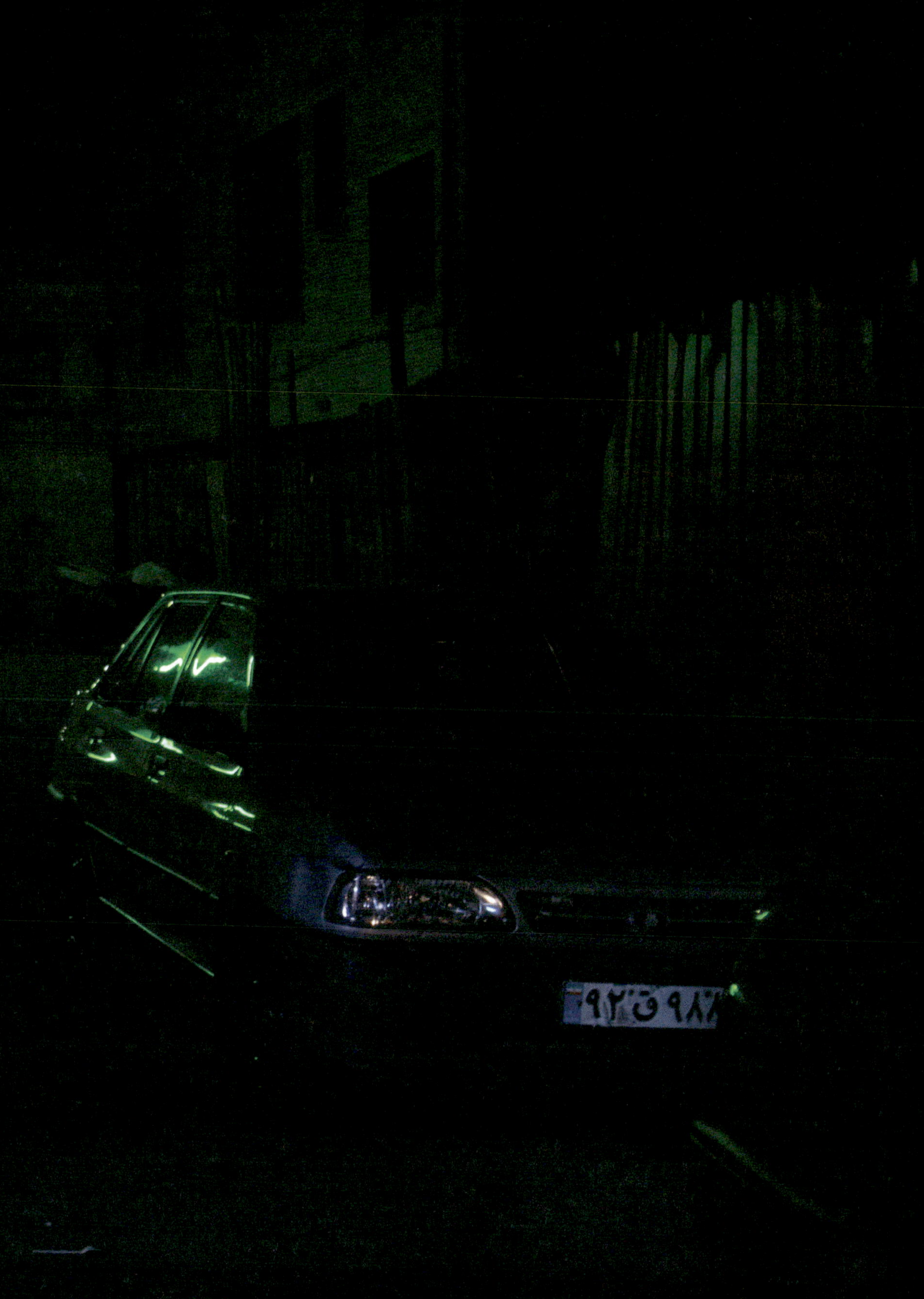
۹۲ ق ۹۸

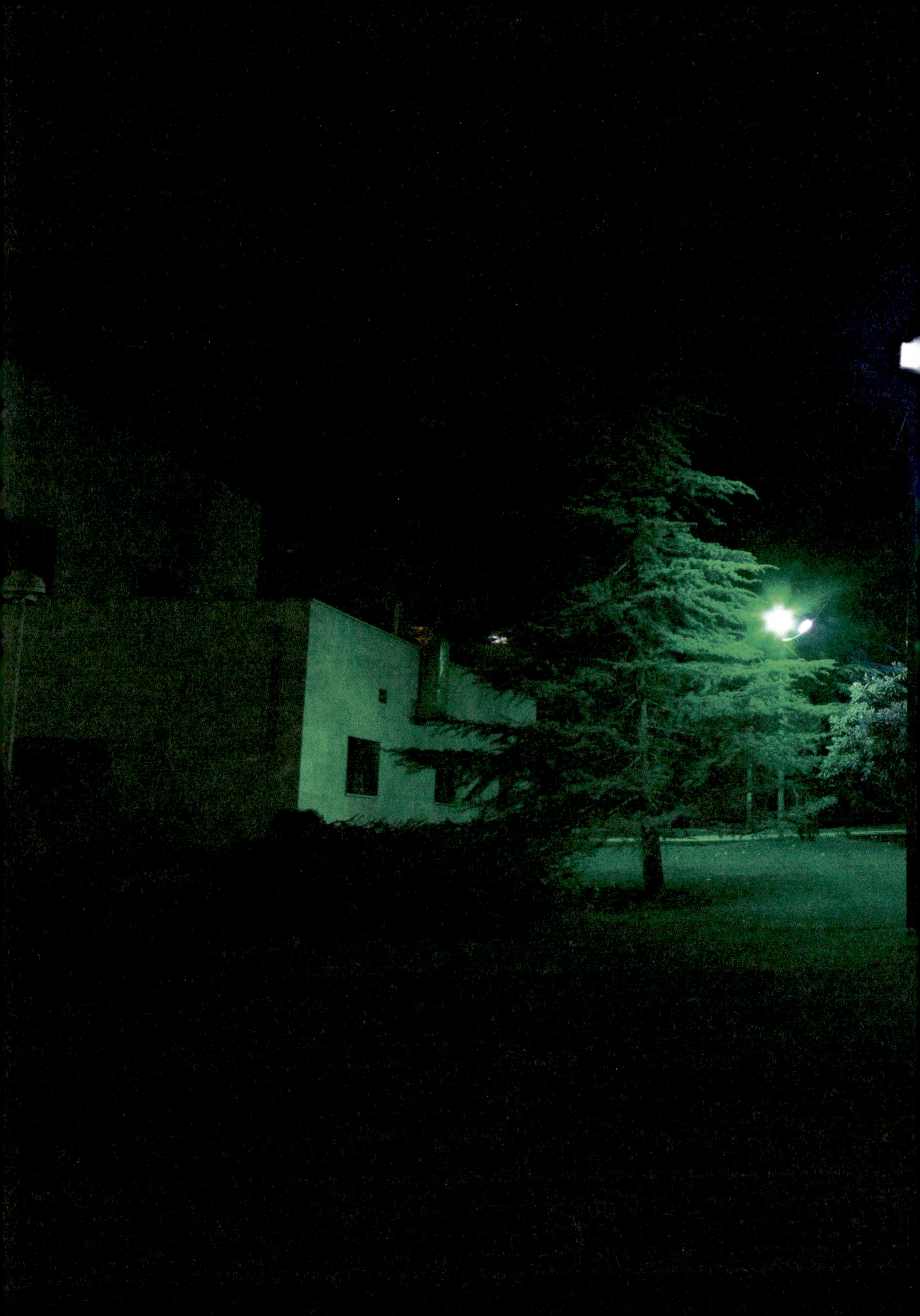

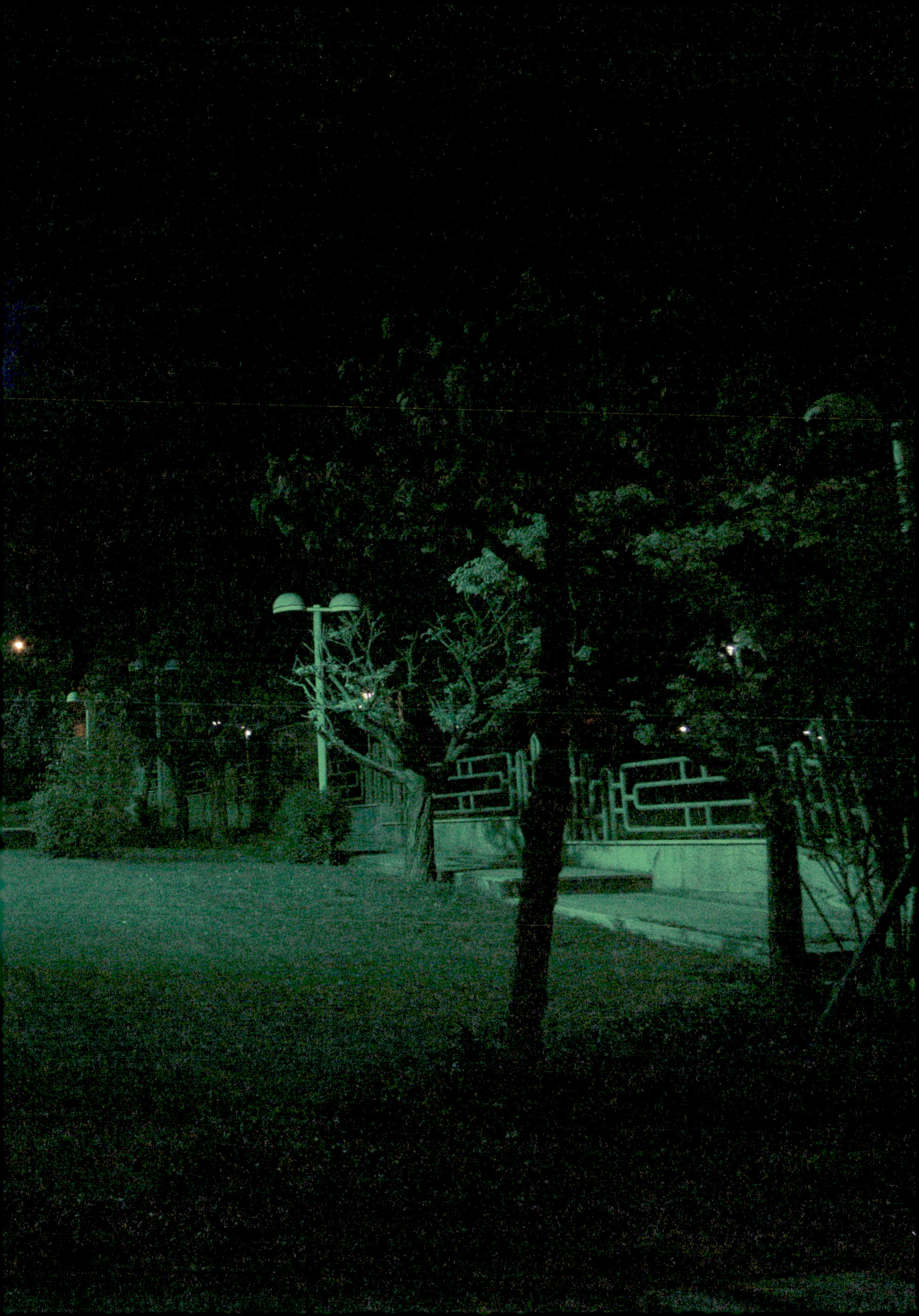

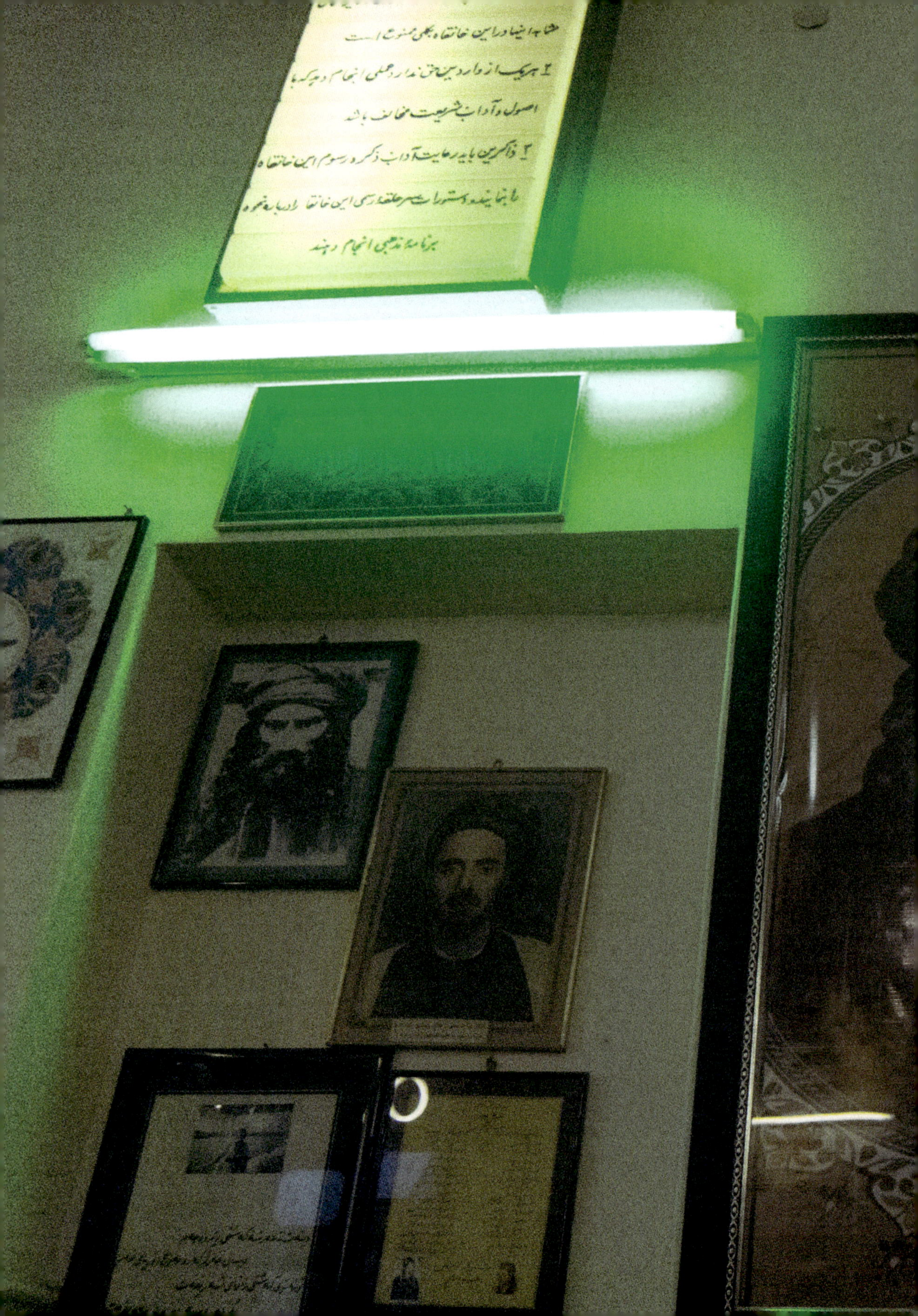
در این خانقاه بکلی ممنوع است
۲ هریک از واردین حق ندارد عملی انجام دهد که با
اصول و آداب شریعت مخالف باشد
۳ ذاکرین باید رعایت آداب ذکر و رسوم این خانقاه
را بنمایند دستورات سرحلقه رسمی این خانقاه را درباره نحوه
برنامه مذهبی انجام دهند

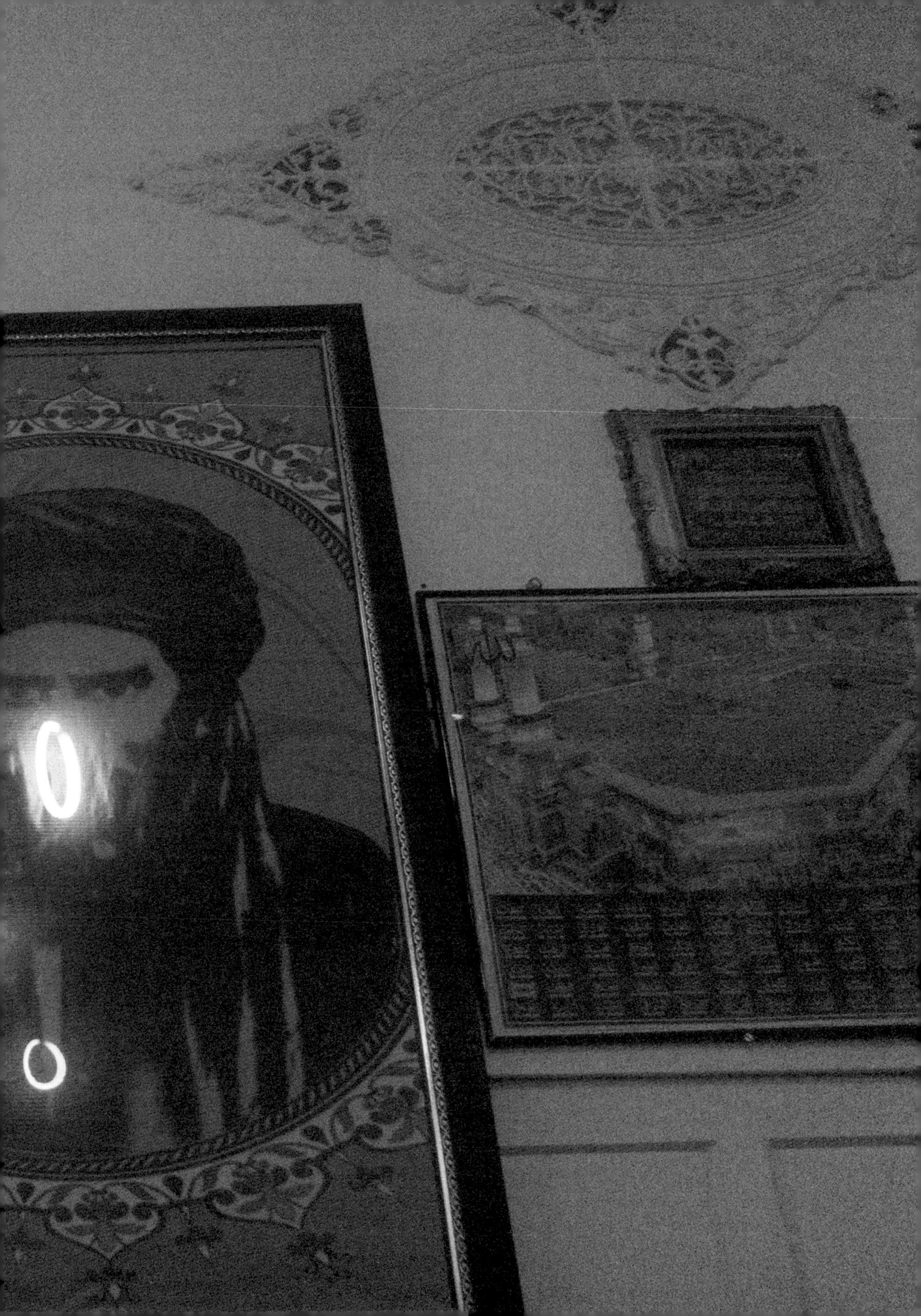

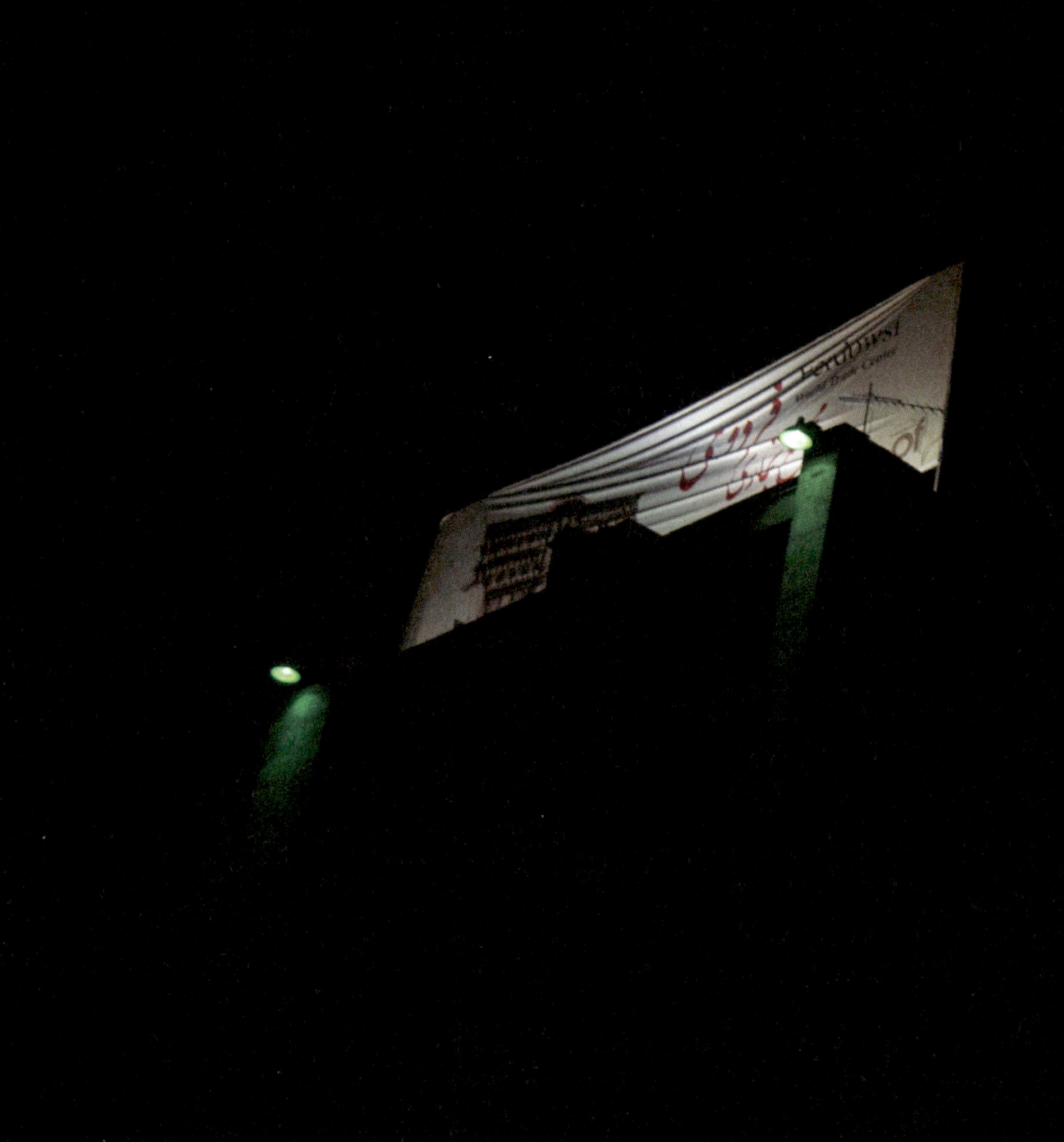

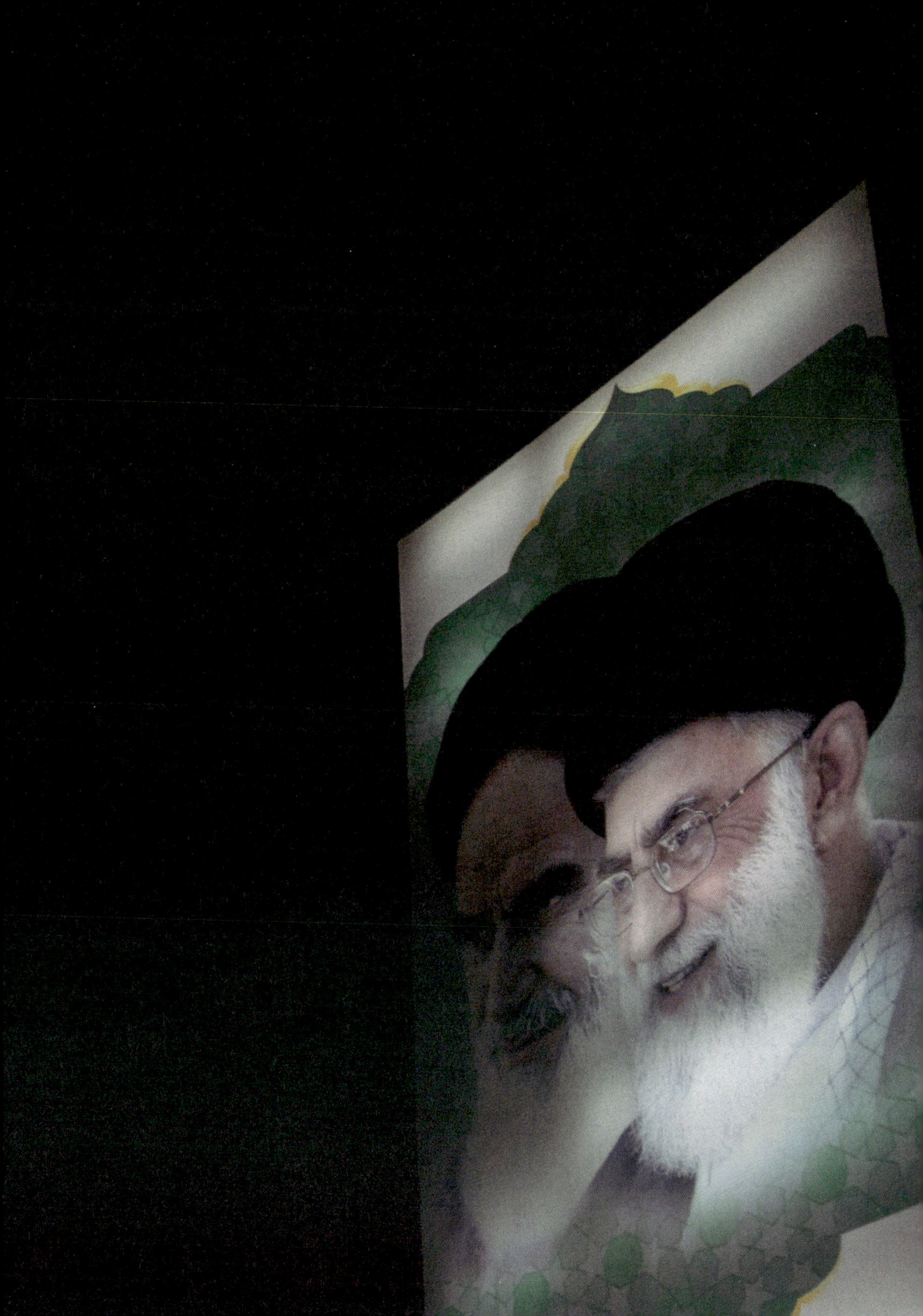

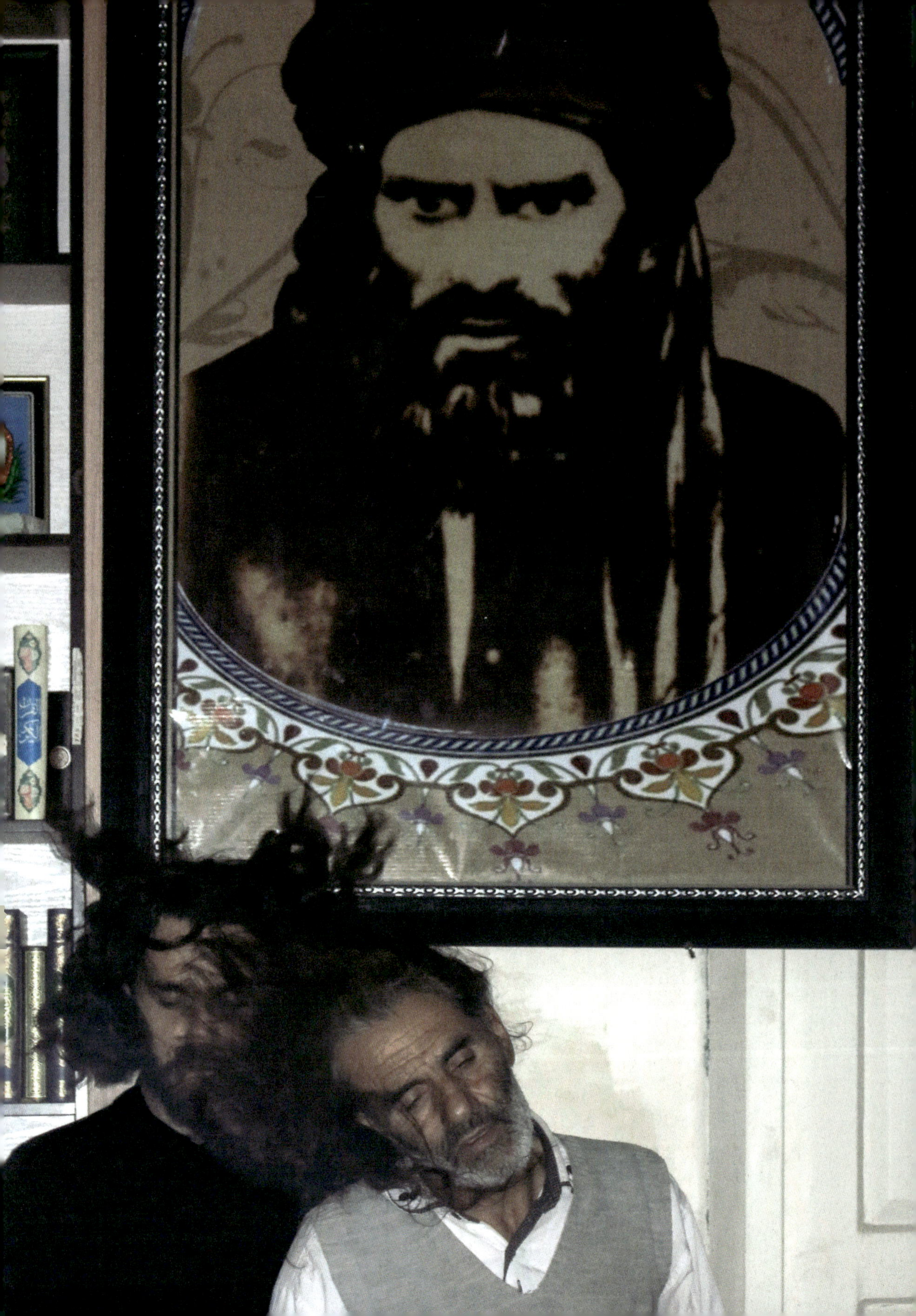

APE#084
Els Vanden Meersch, *Mastering the Curtains*

ISBN 9789490800611
www.artpapereditions.org

Graphic design: Jurgen Maelfeyt (6'56"), Els Vanden Meersch
Translation: Heidi Steffes
Proofreading: Mia Verstraete
Printing: Lannoo, Tielt

First print of 500 copies: February 2017

This book is based on the results of *Mastering The Curtains,* a PhD research project funded by the Royal Academy of Fine Arts Antwerp – AP University College, and published with their support.

ROYAL ACADEMY
OF FINE ARTS
ANTWERP
AP
ARTESIS PLANTIJN
UNIVERSITY COLLEGE

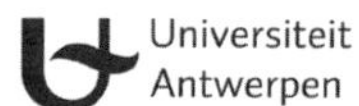

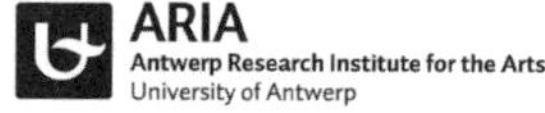